Olive Green:
Learning English
through a Mystery Drama
(CEFR-A2)

CEFR A2

ASARI Yoko
KANNO Satoru
KUBO Takeo
SATO Ryosuke
SIMPSON William

Asahi Press

音声再生アプリ「リスニング・トレーナー」を使った音声ダウンロード

朝日出版社開発のアプリ、「リスニング・トレーナー（リストレ）」を使えば、教科書の音声をスマホ、タブレットに簡単にダウンロードできます。どうぞご活用ください。

◉ アプリ【リスニング・トレーナー】の使い方

《アプリのダウンロード》

App Store または Google Play から「リスニング・トレーナー」のアプリ（無料）をダウンロード

App Storeは
こちら▶

Google Playは
こちら▶

《アプリの使い方》

① アプリを開き「コンテンツを追加」をタップ
② 画面上部に【15683】を入力しDoneをタップ

音声・映像ストリーミング配信 》》》

この教科書の音声及び、付属の映像は、右記ウェブサイトにて無料で配信しています。

https://text.asahipress.com/free/english/

はじめに

　本書は、映画 Olive Green を題材とし、学習者のリスニング能力とスピーキング能力の
さらなる向上を目的として作成されました。この映画は英語学習用に特別に撮り下ろされ、
CEFR に準拠しつつ文法事項が導入されています。この映画を繰り返し視聴することによ
り、学習者は過度な負担を感じることなく、リスニング能力のレベルアップを行うことが
可能となります。

　本書は CEFR の A2 レベルに対応し、A1 レベルに対応する前冊の続きとなる 2 冊目とし
て出版されました。ストーリーも 1 冊目の続きとなります。このため、必要に応じ、受講
生と一緒に 1 冊目に対応する動画をご視聴ください。

　また、各シーンの会話部分のみを録音し直している音源もあり、明瞭な音声で聴きたい
場合やディクテーションの際に活用することができます。

　本書の特徴として、各 Unit のスピーキング練習用のアクティビティが挙げられます。ス
ピーキング・アクティビティは、その Unit で導入された文法項目の学習を意図しています。
ペア・ワーク、グループ・ワークを通し、学習者はスピーキング能力を向上させることが
できます。

　リスニングとスピーキングの 2 つの能力は、日本人学習者にとって苦手とされてきまし
たが、実際の言語使用においては必要不可欠です。また、近年では、多くの英語検定試験
でこの 2 つの能力を測るテストが導入されています。本書を通し、技能向上の一助となる
ことを願っております。

執筆者一同

■各Unitの構成

本書のUnitは主に次のものから成り立っています。

The target of this unit is to understand:

学習する文法事項が最初に示されています。どのような文法事項を学習するのか、初めに確認しておきましょう。

Review Activity

1つ前のUnitで導入された文法事項を復習するためのアクティビティです。主に、ペア・ワークを使ったスピーキング・アクティビティとなっています。

Warm-Up

学習する映画のシーンを見る前に、Warm-Upとして、どの部分に注目すればよいかが導入されています。日本語で2つの質問が書かれていますので、映像を見る前に質問に答えてみましょう。

Let's Watch!

映画のシーンを理解するのに必要となる単語・句・文が掲載されています。あらかじめ発音・意味などを確認しておきましょう。また、この部分には、スクリプトの一部が空欄で提示されています。ディクテーション用のアクティビティとしても活用できます。

Comprehension Check

さまざまな内容確認用の問題を通し、それぞれのシーンの内容を確認することができます。

Grammar

それぞれのUnitで焦点が当てられている文法事項を確認してください。学習する文法事項はCEFRにおおむね準拠しています。

Speaking Activity

スピーキング用のアクティビティが掲載されています。ペア・ワークやグループ・ワークを通し、スピーキングの練習をしていきましょう。

Role Play

Unitの内容と関連する2人の人物の会話が載っています。発展的な内容となっており、シーンでは含めることができなかった単語・表現を練習する機会となります。

Contents

■Main Characters

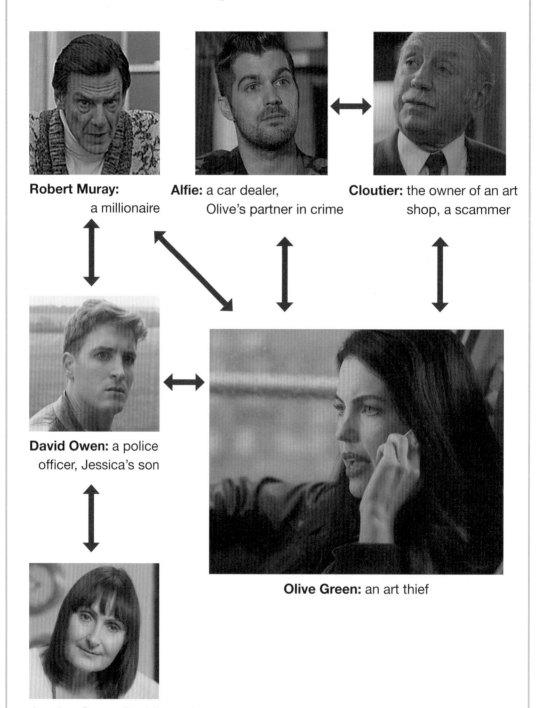

Robert Muray: a millionaire

Alfie: a car dealer, Olive's partner in crime

Cloutier: the owner of an art shop, a scammer

David Owen: a police officer, Jessica's son

Olive Green: an art thief

Jessica Owen: David's mother, the owner of the B&B

Olive Green

Learning English through a Mystery Drama

CEFR-A2

Asahi Press

In the Middle of Nowhere

The target of this unit is to understand:

・Verbs of preference + gerunds/*to* infinitives （動名詞やto不定詞を使った好みを示す表現）

・*How about, Why don't, should*: suggestions （How about, Why don't, shouldを使った文：提案）

Warm-Up

・典型的な日本人のイメージはどのようなものですか？

・普段、朝食にはどんなものを食べますか？

Words and Phrases

CD: Track 02

strong: a strong boxer

tough: He is tough and never afraid.

wake up: wake up early in the morning

soon: I will be back soon.

cover:
The mountain is covered with snow.

hypothermia: die from hypothermia

nasty: I caught a nasty cold.

thoughtful: a thoughtful present

with bare hands:
catch a fish with bare hands

bloody: Oh no! My computer is bloody broken!

admit: admit the fact

deep inside:
Everyone has secrets deep inside.

disagree: disagree on a few points

blanket: a wool blanket

bucket: put the mop in the bucket

spend: spend a week in Vancouver

practically: Smartphones are practically a computer.

holiday: plan a long holiday

insane: insane behavior

keep one's mouth shut: You'd better keep your mouth shut.

socialise (socialize): socialise with people at a party

Frenchman: Cloutier is a Frenchman.

sociable: a sociable child with many friends

hate to say it, but…: I hate to say it, but I don't think you'll pass the class.

feel: feel tired and sleepy

be locked in: The thief was locked in jail.

in the middle of nowhere: I'm lost in the middle of nowhere.

dying: The batteries are dying.

crazy: run away from a crazy man

Brit: Brit is short for British person.

snack: a midnight snack

breakfast: have breakfast at 6:00

candy bar: Candy bars are high calorie.

generally: Mice generally hate cats.

meat: Giraffes never eat meat.

stomach: a pain in my stomach

taste: Coffee tastes bitter.

pass: Can you pass me the salt?

Alfie: How is he doing, Cloutier?

Cloutier: Fine, fine! Marco's a strong, tough, young man. I'm sure he'll
¹(   ) ²(   ) very soon.

Alfie: Yeah, maybe. I still think you should ³(   ) him. Hypothermia is
a ⁴(   ) thing, you know. She's such a ⁵(   ) girl.
Even now, when I want to ... kill Olive with my bare hands, I have to bloody
⁶(   ) ⁷(   ). Deep inside she's a ⁸(   )
and kind person.

Cloutier: Kind? I ⁹(   ). Look at that poor boy.

Alfie: Nah. It's just business. She didn't kill us, did she? She gave us the
¹⁰(   ), food ... even a bucket. We'll be all right. Spend a few days
in the shed, then she'll let us out. It's ¹¹(   ) a holiday.

Cloutier: You are insane, Alfie. Insane. ¹²(   ) ¹³(   )
¹⁴(   ) keep your mouth shut?

Alfie: I can't. I ¹⁵(   ) talking and socialising with people. You are a
Frenchman. Aren't Frenchmen ¹⁶(   ) and ¹⁷(   )?

Cloutier: I hate to say it but I don't feel very sociable right now. Maybe it's because I'm
locked in here, in the ¹⁸(   ) of nowhere, with a dying man and a
crazy Brit.

Alfie: He's not dying. ¹⁹(   ) ²⁰(   ) a snack? We really
should eat something. I believe it's ²¹(   ) time. We've got
some ... well, three ²²(   ) ²³(   ) and some ... ham
²⁴(   ) and some ²⁵(   ) sandwiches.

Cloutier: I'd like a ham sandwich, please. I generally ²⁶(   )
²⁷(   ) start my day with some meat in my stomach.

Alfie: Say ... this tastes kind of funny. Can you ... ²⁸(   ) the bucket,
please?

Comprehension Check

Exercise 1 Who are they?

1.

( )

2.

( )

3.

( )

Exercise 2 True (T) or false (F)?

1. ( ) Marco will die very soon.

2. ( ) Alfie thinks Olive is a nice person.

3. ( ) Cloutier enjoys talking to Alfie.

4. ( ) Cloutier had a cheese sandwich.

5. ( ) Cloutier generally starts his day with some meat.

Exercise 3 Answer the following questions.

1. What is Cloutier's nationality? ( )

2. What is Alfie's nationality? ( )

3. What does Alfie think about Olive?

( )

4. What did Olive give Cloutier, Marco, and Alfie?

( )

Verbs of preference + gerunds/*to* infinitives

love

My mom loves working in her garden. = My mom loves to work in her garden.
My teacher loves teaching English. = My teacher loves to teach English.

like

I like having cereal in the morning. = I like to have cereal in the morning.
You really like dancing. = You really like to dance.

prefer

They don't like tea. They prefer drinking coffee. = They prefer to drink coffee.
My family prefers living in big cities. = My family prefers to live in big cities.

hate

I hate telling lies. = I hate to tell lies.
We hate flying long hours. = We hate to fly long hours.

How about, Why don't, should: suggestions

How about + noun or *-ing*

How about a snack?
How about playing outside?

Why don't + *you/we* + verb

You look tired. Why don't you go to bed early?
This homework is so difficult. Why don't we work together after school?

should + verb

We should eat something! We haven't eaten since yesterday.
You should visit Tokyo! It's a really exciting city.

Exercise 1 Fill in the blanks by changing the forms of the verbs in ( ).

e.g., *My father likes literature. He (**loves reading**/**loves to read**) poetry. (love, read)*

1. My mother is an excellent baker. She (   ) cakes. (like, make)
2. You are not active. You (   ) at home. (prefer, stay)
3. Please finish your meal. I (   ) food. (hate, waste)
4. My classmates love this class. They (   ) English. (love, practice)
5. We (   ) films at home. (prefer, watch)

Exercise 2 Complete the sentences with *How about, Why don't we,* or *should*.

1. A: I'm tired and hungry.
   B: (   ) order pizza?
2. A: Let's go somewhere sunny and tropical!
   B: (   ) Bali? It has beautiful beaches.
3. A: I think it will rain this evening.
   B: We (   ) take an umbrella to be safe.
4. A: Who should be the group leader?
   B: (   ) Paul. He is very experienced.

Exercise 3 Reorder the words to make a sentence.

1. Sam (school / going / to / hates).
   (   )
2. Naomi (shopping / go / to / likes) on Sundays.
   (   )
3. Tod (the river / catching / in / fish / loved) in his youth.
   (   )
4. My parents (countryside / in / living / prefer / the) to living in the city.
   (   )

TASK: Suggesting a job for your partners

You are going to suggest a good job for your partners.

Step 1: Add eight more jobs to the list below.

police officer		
accountant		
lawyer		
firefighter		

Step 2: Ask your partners the following questions. Put a ✔ in the chart. Add more information.

		Partner 1		Partner 2	
		☺	☹	☺	☹
1	Do you like being active?				
2	Do you like to lead?				
3	Do you prefer to stay indoors?				
4	Do you like working with computers?				
5	Do you like to be creative?				
6	Do you love helping people?				
7	Do you prefer to work as a team?				
8	Do you love talking to people?				
9	Ask a question: ( )				

Step 3: Discuss the best job for each person.

Useful Expressions

(a) Giving opinions and giving reasons
I think you/he/she should be ... because you/he/she like(s) ...
Maybe you/he/she should not be ... because you/he/she hate(s) ...
How about ...? You/He/She like(s) ...

(b) Asking for opinions
Do you agree?
What do you think?

(c) Agreeing and disagreeing
That's a good idea!
I agree with you.
I think so too.
I don't think so.
I'm not sure about that.

Role Play

CD: Track 05

Listen and fill in the blanks.

Daiki: Jimin, do you like $_1$_____?

Jimin: Yes, I'm very active. I like $_2$_____. I especially love

$_3$_____.

Camila: Do you like $_4$_____?

Jimin: Not really. I am shy.

Daiki: Okay. Do you prefer $_5$_____?

Jimin: I prefer $_6$_____. I don't like $_7$_____.

....

Jimin: What do you think is a good job for me?

Daiki: Well, I think you should $_8$_____ because you like to help people.
What do you think, Camila?

Camila: Hmm... I'm not sure about that. Jimin prefers $_9$_____. How about
$_{10}$_____? She can show wonderful places in Japan to foreign
tourists.

Daiki: That's a good idea! She likes $_{11}$_____ and $_{12}$_____.
It's perfect.

Jimin: Thank you, everyone.

Unit 2

Blackmail

The target of this unit is to understand:

・*Be going to*: future（be going to を含む文：未来）
・*Will*: future（will を含む文：未来）
・Present continuous: future（現在進行形を含む文：未来）
・Possessive pronouns (*mine, yours*, etc.)（所有代名詞）

Review Activity

ペアになって次の活動が好きかどうかお互い英語で尋ねてみましょう。

・like, love, don't like, hate などを使いましょう。
・嫌いなものに関しては、How about ...?, Why don't you ...?, You should ...を使って、アドバイスしましょう。

e.g.,   A: *Do you like going shopping?*   A: *Do you like going shopping?*
            B: *Yes, I love going shopping.*   B: *No, I hate going shopping.*
                                          A: *Why don't you shop online?*

go shopping	get up early
eat vegetables	give a presentation
play video games	cook meals

Warm-Up

1. 誰かに弱みをにぎられたことはありますか？
2. 人を手助けしたことはありますか？ どんなことをしましたか？

Scene 2-1

Words and Phrases

situation: a difficult situation

serious: serious injuries

remember: remember her name

last night: I ate roast beef for dinner last night.

get ... wrong:
I got two questions wrong in my test.

do research on:
The doctor does research on cancer.

professional: a professional artist

cold: a cold and angry boss

calculating: a clever and calculating lawyer

far: She is far nicer than other people.

confidential: confidential information

data: scientific data

get back: Did you get your money back?

in fact:
It's cold. In fact, it's practically winter.

conversation: make light conversation with her

sergeant: She became a sergeant.

(police) station: go to the police station for help

certainly: She is certainly smart.

enemy: fight with the enemy

destroy: destroy the toy castle

make a mistake: make a careless mistake on the test

spoil: spoil a surprise birthday party

Script of the Scene

Robert: So, David, this situation with Olive ... it's very serious. What are we gonna do about it?

David: I don't know that, but I do [1](   ) you tried to kill me [2](   ) [3](   ).

Robert: Did I? You got that wrong. You see, I've done some research on Miss Green. She's a [4](   ) art thief. Cold, [5](   ) woman ...

David: Last night, did she steal one of your [6](   )?

Robert: No, she did something far worse. She [7](   ) some confidential business [8](   ). So I need you to find her and get it back.

David: No way. No way. [9](   ) [10](   ), after this conversation, I'm [11](   ) my sergeant at the station to tell him everything about you ...

Robert : You're certainly not! Olive's [12](   ) my enemies destroy me and my business. And you helped her. What's your sergeant [13](   ) do with you? You made a mistake. But you're a good policeman. Don't spoil that. So ... [14](   ) you [15](   ) me?

 Words and Phrases

Forget it.: Forget it. I'll do it myself.

promise: keep a promise

be careful with: Be careful with the hot water.

extra: extra large coffee

former: the former president

associate: do business with my associates

one more thing: There's one more thing. Can you also wash the dishes?

get into debt: He got into debt because he lost his job.

enormous: an enormous castle

guest house: stay at the guest house

Script of the Scene

CD: Track 10, 11 / DVD: Chapter 03 (03:10-05:58)

David: Forget it.

Robert: If you don't find her, my friends ¹⁶(   ). And they ¹⁷(   )
be nice to her. I can promise you that.

David: ¹⁸(   ) ¹⁹(   ). I'll do it.

Robert: Use this. It's a ²⁰(   ) ²¹(   ). We must be extra
careful with Miss Green. And here are the names and addresses of her former
²²(   ). Start there. And ²³(   ) ²⁴(   )
²⁵(   ). It's sad, but your mum's got into debt. ²⁶(   )
debt. Did you know that? Her little guest house can be ²⁷(   ) even
tomorrow, so ... need I say more?

Comprehension Check

Exercise 1 Who are they?

1.

(   )

2.

(   )

Exercise 2 True (T) or false (F)?

1. (   ) David doesn't remember anything about last night.
2. (   ) Robert asked David to help him find Olive.
3. (   ) David will tell his sergeant about Robert later.
4. (   ) David will not help Robert.
5. (   ) David's mom's B&B is very successful.

Exercise 3 Answer the following questions.

1. What is Olive's last name?   (   )
2. What is Olive's job?   (   )
3. What did Olive steal from Robert? (   )
4. What did Robert give David?   (   )
5. Why is David's mother in trouble? (   )

Grammar

Be going to

→ intention for the near future

I'm going to watch TV after school.

→ plans made previously

I am going to travel to Spain with my family this summer.

→ predictions based on facts and evidence

We broke our mother's favorite vase. She's going to be very angry!

Will

→ decisions that are made immediately

My car is not here. – Don't worry, we will give you a lift.

→ future activities in general

The laptop is completely broken! I will not finish work on time!

→ opinions, hopes, expectations (with such verbs as: *think, hope, expect, be sure*, etc.)

Will the weather be nice tomorrow? -It won't. It'll rain, I think.

Present continuous

> **→ planned arrangement or actions in the near future**

We can't meet on Friday. We are leaving New York then.
I'm telling Mom what you did.
My teacher isn't coming to school today because he's got a serious cold.

Possessive pronouns (*mine, yours* etc.)

This is my book.   → This is mine.
This is your car.   → This is yours.
This is his/her ball. → This is his/hers.
This is our place.   → This is ours.
This is their manor. → This is theirs.

Exercise 1   **Fill in the blanks with the present continuous form of the verbs in ( ).**

1. Let's go to bed early today. The plane (   ) at 8:00 a.m. tomorrow. (leave)
2. (   ) you (   ) my mom about what I've done to you? Please, don't! (tell)

Exercise 2   **Fill in the blanks with *will* and the verbs in ( ).**

1. Your bag looks heavy. Here, I (   ) you. (help)
2. The car is completely broken, it (   ) this time. (not start)

Exercise 3   **Fill in the blanks with *be going to* and the verbs in ( ).**

1. Who (   ) to the party tomorrow evening? I sent the letters to everyone in our English class. (come)
2. According to the weather forecast, it (   ) a beautiful sunny weekend.

(be)

Exercise 4   **Choose the form which best fits the context.**

1. A: Any plans for tonight?
   B: Yeah, I (am going to visit / will visit) my grandparents.
2. *Ring ... Ring ...*
   A: Someone's calling!
   B: (I'm going to get / I'll get) it.
3. A: Let's go out for lunch.
   B: Sorry I can't. (I'm seeing / I'll see) a client in ten minutes.
4. A: Did you tell Saki about Ken's birthday this Friday?
   B: Oops, I forgot. (I'm going to call / I'll call) her now.

Exercise 5 Fill in the blanks with a possessive pronoun.

e.g., This is Tom's pen. It's (his).

1. These are my brothers' toys. They are (   ).

2. The bag belongs to Sarah. It's (   ).

3. We were here first. This parking space is (   ).

4. A: There are two cups here. Which one is (   )?

    B: This one is my cup, so that one.

5. A: Excuse me, I think you have my luggage.

    B: Sorry, is it (   )? Let me check.

Speaking Activity

TASK: Making a travel plan

Your group won a free trip to one of the following cities. You have five days. You must travel in February. Talk with the members of your group and decide on a travel destination.

Step 1: Read the description below about the three cities.

Phuket, Thailand

Weather:	Sunny, 28 °C
Attractions:	marine activities like snorkeling and diving
Food:	tropical fruits, Thai curry, fresh seafood
Accommodation:	4-star resort hotel with a private beach
Distance from Tokyo:	About 8 hours

Paris, France

Weather:	Rainy and cloudy, 5 °C
Attractions:	visiting museums, shopping at Champs Elysee
Food:	croissants and baguettes
Accommodation:	3-star hotel with a view of the Eiffel Tower
Distance from Tokyo:	About 12 hours

Rio de Janeiro, Brazil

Weather:	Humid with rain, 25 °C
Attractions:	watching soccer games, Copacabana Beach
Food:	Brazilian barbecue
Accommodation:	5-star hotel by the Copacabana Beach, a suite on the top floor
Distance from Tokyo:	About 24 hours

Step 2: Choose the city you want to go to. Give your opinions and ask for opinions.

Useful Expressions

(a) Giving opinions and making suggestions

I'd like to go somewhere (hot / cold / tropical). How about (Paris / Phuket / Rio de Janeiro)?

Why don't we go to (Paris / Phuket / Rio de Janeiro) ?

(b) Asking opinions

Where do you want to go?

What will we do?

(c) Agreeing and disagreeing

That's a good idea! It sounds (exciting / dangerous / delicious / like fun).

I'm not sure about that.

Step 3: Present to your class <u>three things</u> your group will do during your stay. Use the information in Step 1.

e.g, Making plans

We will We're going to	try a local food relax at go out to eat go shopping visit a museum enjoy the hotel hang out at a private beach

Listen and fill in the blanks.

CD: Track 12

Jimin: So, I want to go to 1 _____ because I want to 2 _____.

Daiki: Me too. I also love 3 _____, so why don't we go to

4 _____?

Camila: Hmm... I'm sorry I disagree. I hate cold weather. I prefer travelling to

5 _____ to travelling to 6 _____.

How about 7 _____? I love 8 _____ and I want to

9 _____. I think, it is called Churrasco.

We'll be able to 10 _____.

Jimin: Oh yes. You are right, Camila. Maybe it'll be 11 _____ in February.

What do you think, Daiki?

Daiki: Rio de Janeiro is too far. It's going to 12 _____. Why don't we

go to 13 _____ then? We'll try 14 _____. We'll have

15 _____.

Camila: That's a good idea. It sounds exciting.

Jimin: Okay. Then we will go to 16 _____.

Home Sweet Home

The target of this unit is to understand:

・Present simple: schedules and habitual activities（現在形を含む文：スケジュールと習慣的行為）

Review Activity

次の表はオーランド（Orlando）の次の日曜日の予定を示したものです。彼の予定を英語で表してみましょう。

11:00 AM	meet a friend
12:00 PM	lunch at a restaurant
1:30 PM	watch a movie
4:00 PM	go home
7:00 PM	dinner
8:30 PM	read a book
11:30 PM	go to bed

Warm-Up

1. 両親に嘘をついたことはありますか。それはどんな嘘ですか。
2. 仮病で休んだことはありますか。

Scene 3-1

Words and Phrases

🔊 CD: Track 13

uniform: wear a school uniform

take the day off: My father took a day off
from work.

sick: She's been sick since last week.

hangover: have a little hangover from last
night's party

plain: plain yoghurt

gosh: Gosh, it's so hot today.

fry-up:
The bed and breakfast serves fry-ups.

bacon: a thin slice of bacon

appointment:
make a dentist's appointment

borrow: borrow a book

What's wrong with ...?: What's wrong with
the printer? It's not working.

Script of the Scene

🔊 CD: Track 14, 15 / DVD: Chapter 04 (05:59-06:45)

Jessica: You're not wearing your uniform? You ¹(   ) work at 8 a.m.
You'll be late.

David: I've taken the ²(   ) ³(   ).

Jessica: The day off? Are you ⁴(   )? Hangover? If it's a ⁵(   )
⁶(   ), gosh, tea and a fry-up will make you feel better.
I'll fry some eggs and bacon, okay?

David: I'm not sick, it's not a hangover. I just ... have an important ⁷(   ) in
London today. And I need to borrow your car to get there.

Jessica: My car? What's wrong with ⁸(   )?

🌿 Words and Phrases

lend: lend 10,000 yen to a friend

Here's the thing.: Here's the thing. I love her.

all of a sudden: All of a sudden, the lights turned off.

miserable: a miserable life

get over: My friend can't get over his ex.

silly face: make a silly face in the picture

be gone: My phone is gone.

suddenly: Suddenly, it began to rain.

mean: Red light means stop.

complicated: This complicated problem is hard to solve.

at least: It's so hot. It's at least 35 ℃.

be worth: This painting is worth a million dollars.

doubt: I doubt that she is a thief.

soon enough: People will find out the truth soon enough.

🌿 Script of the Scene

🔊 CD: Track 17, 18 / DVD: Chapter 05 (06:46-07:51)

David: Olive's got it.

Jessica: You mean you've ^{9}(   ) ^{10}(   ) to her or she has ^{11}(   ) ^{12}(   )?

David: She's stolen it. Okay ... ^{13}(   ) ^{14}(   ) ^{15}(   )

Jessica: I don't want to know. Really, I don't. First, you two ^{16}(   ) dating, then all of a sudden you ^{17}(   ). And you're so miserable. And I think "Okay, she's just a girl, ^{18}(   ) get over it. And a few days later, you're sitting here with a silly face, your car's gone, and suddenly your work ^{19}(   ) ^{20}(   ) anything to you.

David: It's more complicated than that. Mum, are you ^{21}(   ) ^{22}(   ) give me your car or not? I need to know now because the bus ^{23}(   ) in 20 minutes or so.

Jessica: All right, all right. Is she at least worth it?

David: I ^{24}(   ) ^{25}(   ), but I'll know soon enough.

Comprehension Check

Exercise 1 Who is this woman? What is her relationship with David?

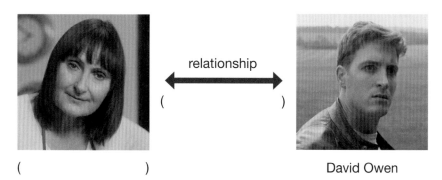

relationship

(   )

(   )

David Owen

Exercise 2 True (T) or false (F)?

1. (   ) David has a hangover.
2. (   ) David gave Olive his car.
3. (   ) Jessica will lend her car to David.
4. (   ) David and Olive are a couple.

Exercise 3 Answer the following questions.

1. What does David say he has to do in London?

   (   )

2. What does Jessica say is good for a hangover?

   (   )

3. Why is Jessica worried about David?

   (   )

4. Why is David in a hurry?

   (   )

Grammar

Present simple

→ **fixed schedules**

English classes start at 9 a.m. on Mondays and Fridays.

A: Excuse me, I'd like to get to London. What time does the train leave?

B: The next train leaves at 10:05.

→ **habitual activities**

Typical time expressions:

always, usually, sometimes, never, every day, every week, on weekends, on Mondays

My sister runs every morning and does some exercises every other day.

I listen to classical music on my father's record player.

My teacher wears his favorite navy tie to church.

Exercise 1 **Complete the sentences with the verbs in the box. Make sure to change the verbs to the correct form if necessary. You can use each word only once.**

leave	run	go	come	have

1. The train to Notre Dame (   ) from Track 11.

2. I (   ) an appointment with my dentist at 4:00 today.

3. John (   ) about 20 kilometers on weekends.

4. My grandparents usually (   ) to our house for New Year's.

5. My mother (   ) to a café to study French every morning before work.

Exercise 2 Look at the table and answer the questions.

Flight #	Departure Gate	Departure City	Arriving City	Departure Time	Arrival Time
CA 986	13	San Francisco (SFO)	Beijing (PEK)	2:50 PM	5:55 PM (next day)
CA 655	2	Shanghai (PVG)	Tokyo (TKO)	11:25 AM	4:00 PM
CA 985	4	Beijing (PEK)	Shanghai (PVG)	10:30 AM	1:00 PM
CA 881	27	New York (JFK)	Phuket (HKT)	4:30 PM	6:15 PM (next day)

1. What time does the flight from Shanghai leave to Tokyo?

(   )

2. Which flight arrives at Beijing?

(   )

3. How long does the flight from Beijing to Shanghai take?

(   )

4. From which gate does CA881 depart?

(   )

5. Which city does flight CA655 arrive at?

(   )

Exercise 3 Reorder the words to make a sentence.

1. He (coffee / never / midnight / drinks / after).

He (   ).

2. Does (before / breakfast / father / newspaper / read / the / your)?

Does (   )?

3. My brother (I / Sundays / and / don't / get / early / on / up).

My brother (   ).

Exercise 4 Answer the following questions.

1. What do you sometimes do with your friends on Friday nights?

(   )

2. What do you and your family usually do for New Year's?

(   )

TASK: Talking about routines and usual activities

Work in pairs. Find out what your partner usually does on New Year's, Christmas, etc. Ask them: "What do you usually do (for) ...?" Use the **Useful Expressions** to help you answer your partner's questions.

Your Partner's Yearly Schedule

	Events	Activities
1	New Year's holiday	
2	Christmas	
3	Summer vacation	
4	Your birthday	
5	On weekends	

Useful Expressions

e.g., I (usually, always, sometimes) ...

go on a trip	cook traditional dishes
have a party	bake cakes
go out to eat	go to the beach
hang out with friends	go camping
watch fireworks	visit grandparents
get presents	go to an amusement park

Listen and fill in the blanks.

Jimin: Daiki, every year, what do you usually do for 1 _____?

Daiki: I love New Year's holiday. My mother cooks 2 _____. You know, *osechi*. We take that to my grandparents' house. My grandparents give my brother and me some 3 _____. How about you?

Jimin: I usually go to 4 _____, too. They live in Osaka. We always eat a lot of 5 _____! I usually put on weight.

Daiki: Me too! What do you usually do during 6 _____?

Jimin: I usually 7 _____. I have a part time job. I 8 _____ so I can hang out with my friends. What about you?

Daiki: My family and I sometimes 9 _____. Last year, we went to Germany. It was really fun! This year, we will go to Spain.

Jimin: Wow! You're so lucky!

[Unit **4**]

Negotiations

The target of this unit is to understand:

・*May / Could*: permission and possibility（may / couldを含む文：許可と可能性）
・*Shall I ...? / Shall we ...?*: polite offers and suggestions（Shallを含む文：丁寧な申し出と提案）

Review Activity

ペアを組み、次のことを英語で話しましょう。

・あなたが普段日常的にやっていること。（現在形を使って）
・最近夢中になってやっていること。（現在進行形を使って）

Warm-Up

1. 買い物のとき、法外な値段を請求された経験はありますか？
2. 自分は交渉上手だと思いますか？

Scene 4-1

 Words and Phrases

🔊 CD: Track 20

deliver: deliver a package

catch a flight:
catch a connecting flight at LA

It's not going to happen.: I'm going to marry the Prince of England one day.
– No way, it's not going to happen.

take precautions:
take precautions against disasters

mess up: mess up the plan

be up to something: Don't trust her. She's up to something.

Like what?: Let's do something fun!
– Like what?

Script of the Scene

🔊 CD: Track 21, 22 / DVD: Chapter 06 (07:52-08:36)

Olive: I want to deliver the thing today. Today! I could still catch an afternoon flight to ¹( ) ²( ).

Client: It's not going to happen. I ³( ) need to take precautions because you ⁴( ) ⁵( ) the job in Old Berry. The police are not doing anything, but Robert Murray ⁶( ) ⁷( ) up to something.

Olive: ⁸( ) ⁹( )?

Client: There are things I haven't told you about him. ¹⁰( ) ¹¹( ), just find a safe place and stay there.

Scene 4-2

 Words and Phrases

🔊 CD: Track 23

park: the police car parked behind the building

grand: cost ten grand

damned: Don't give me your damned excuses.

heartless: heartless words

opportunity: a good opportunity to speak English

cash: pay in cash

sedan: a black sedan

It's a deal: I'll help you if you help me.
– It's a deal.

refreshments: get some refreshments for the party

quid: A quid is a pound.

Alfie: So, may I know what went wrong?

Olive: No, you ¹²(   ) ¹³(   ). Look, I need a clean car. Nothing big, but I need it ¹⁴(   ).

Alfie: Not a problem. You may have one of the two parked at the back. They are ¹⁵(   ) grand each.

Olive: Five thousand of your damned British ¹⁶(   )? You usually take ¹⁷(   ) ¹⁸(   ).

Alfie: Yes, but I can tell that you're deep in trouble, which for me is a great business opportunity.

Olive: You heartless bastard. I don't have that much ¹⁹(   ) on me.

Olive: I could ²⁰(   ) ²¹(   ) 2k and add the sedan parked outside.

Alfie: I don't like the colour, but ... all right. ²²(   ) ²³(   ) ²⁴(   ).

....

Alfie: Good. Business is done, so it's time for refreshments. ²⁵(   ) ²⁶(   ) make you some tea? Coffee? Shall I get you ²⁷(   ) to eat?

Olive: That would be great. How much for the food? A thousand quid?

Comprehension Check

Exercise 1 Who is Olive talking to on the phone?

Exercise 2 True (T) or false (F)?

1. (   ) Olive messed up her job in New York.

2. (   ) The client allowed Olive to go back to America.

3. (   ) Olive sold the sedan to Alfie.

4. (   ) Alfie will receive five thousand pounds from Olive.

Exercise 3 Answer the following questions.

1. Where does the client advise Olive to stay?

   (   )

2. What does Olive want from Alfie?

   (   )

3. What was the deal?

   (   )

4. Is Olive happy with the deal? Why or why not?

   (   )

Grammar

May / Could

→ **permission**

May / Could I come in? -Yes, you may.

May / Could I watch some TV after dinner? – No, you may not.

→ **possibility**

– Do you want to go out with me this weekend?

– Sorry, I may / could be busy. I have to study for an exam.

Shall I ...? / Shall we ...?

→ **polite offers (*Shall I ...?*)**

Are you hungry? Shall I make you some sandwiches?

Those bags look heavy. Shall I help you?

→ **suggestions (*Shall we ...?*)**

Shall we go to Italy this summer?

It's noon already. Shall we have lunch?

Exercise 1 **Fill in the blanks with *May I, Shall I, or Shall we.***

1. A: Happy birthday, Yuki.

   B: (   ) open the presents?

   A: Of course you can. I hope you like it.

2. A: (   ) go to an amusement park this weekend?

   B: Yes, let's. I love roller coasters.

3. A: Hi, Tom. I'm making some sandwiches for myself now. (   ) make some for you?

   B: Yes, please. Thank you.

Exercise 2 Read the following situations. Ask for permission (*May I ...?*), give suggestions (*Shall we ...?*), or offer help (*Shall I ...?*).

1. You see an old woman with a suitcase. She needs to go up the stairs. What would you say?

   Shall I (   )?

2. You and your friend are going out for dinner. You know a very good Italian restaurant. What would you say?

   Shall we (   )?

3. You see someone wearing very interesting clothes, so you want to take a photo of them. What would you say to them?

   May I (   )?

Exercise 3 Look at the picture. Use *may* or *could* to answer the questions.

1. What does the weather look like?

   (   )

2. What's wrong with the girl?

   (   )

TASK: Coming up with a plan

You are going to spend a week on a deserted island with the members of your group. You must decide which **three things** you will take with you.

Step 1: Label the items.

1. (   )
protect from the sun

2. (   )
sleep comfortably

3. (   )
have a shelter

4. (   )
see in the dark

5. (   )
contact people

6. (   )
start a fire

7. (   )
go swimming

8. (   )
kill bugs

9. (   )
find direction

10. (   )
cut meat

11. (   )
wash yourself

12. (   )
eat

Step 2: Decide which **three items** you should take with your group.

Useful Expressions

(a) Making predictions
We could get ... There may be .... It could be .... Maybe there won't be .... It may (rain / get very hot / etc.).

(b) Making suggestions

Why don't we take a ...?
Shall we choose ...?
How about bringing ...?
I think we should choose ... because ...

(c) Agreeing and disagreeing

Do you agree?
What do you think?
I don't think so.
I'm not sure about that.
I see your point.

Step 3: **Tell your class which items your group chose. What was the most popular item? What was the least popular?**

🔊 **CD: Track 26**

Listen and fill in the blanks.

Daiki: Okay, so I think we should definitely take a $_1$ _____ . It may

$_2$ _____ and we need a shelter. What do you think, everyone?

Jimin: Yes, I agree. Why don't we take $_3$ _____ . We need food. There may

not be $_4$ _____ on the island.

Camila: Hmm. I'm not sure about that. Maybe we could $_5$ _____ or

$_6$ _____ . We may not need $_7$ _____ .

Daniel: Camila, I see your point. Okay, shall we bring $_8$ _____ ? I can't live

without my phone.

Jimin: Daniel, you're kidding. $_9$ _____ will probably die, and we will

not be able to charge them. We don't need our phones.

Daiki: Daniel, I'm sorry, but I agree with Jimin. How about bringing

$_{10}$ _____ ? It may be $_{11}$ _____ at night.

Camila: I agree. Okay, so we will definitely take $_{12}$ _____ and

$_{13}$ _____ . Does everyone agree?

Jimin: Yes. So we can only choose one more thing.

Visiting Cloutier

The target of this unit is to understand:

・*Have / Has to* and *must* in positive sentences（肯定文のhave/has to, must）

・*Don't have to* vs. *must not / mustn't*（don't have toとmust not / mustn'tの対比）

・*Someone / Something*, etc.（不定代名詞）

Review Activity

次の状況をmay/couldを使って説明してみましょう。そのあと、Shall I ...? を使って声をかけてみましょう。

Warm-Up

1. 警察官に声をかけられたことはありますか？

2. 違法行為を見かけたらどうしますか？

Scene 5-1

Words and Phrases

 CD: Track 27

village: a small quiet village

splendid: a splendid idea

beauty: the natural beauty of the country

female: a female driver

favourite (favorite): favourite movies

canvas: paint a picture on a canvas

frame: a large frame for the picture

original: an original painting by Van Gogh

fairly: It can get fairly hot in the summer.

inexpensive: an inexpensive gift

disappointed: I am disappointed with my test score.

upset: She was upset about the news.

giant: a giant company

almost: almost the whole day

metre (meter): run 100 metres in ten seconds

height: I'm afraid of heights.

truly: I am truly sorry.

impressive: That singer's voice is impressive.

plaster: a plaster figure

Script of the Scene

CD: Track 28, 29 / DVD: Chapter 08 (10:24-12:07)

Cloutier: *Three Village Girls by the Stream* [1](   ) Francesco Mazzini. Splendid, isn't it? The beauty of the female body was his [2](   ) topic. Oil on canvas, 70 by 50 cm. The wood frame is not original. [3](   ) [4](   ) [5](   ) it is fairly inexpensive. Only 15 thousand pounds. You're disappointed? I understand. But you [6](   ) be upset. I have something less expensive you may like. [7](   ) [8](   ) *The Power of Man*!

David: But it looks like a .... No, it *is* a giant ...

Cloutier: Yes. Almost [9](   ) metres in height. Truly impressive. But it's [10](   ) [11](   ) cheap plaster. Now, tell me ... [12](   ) [13](   ) [14](   ) want?

David: Olive Green. I [15](   ) find her. I know you two worked together in the past. If you know where she is, you [16](   ) [17](   ) tell me.

Cloutier: Two things, my young friend. First, I don't have to do [18](   ). Second, I don't know [19](   ) with that name.

 **Words and Phrases**

CD: Track 30

lie: tell a lie

colleague: a business colleague

Sir: May I take your order, sir?

respectable: a respectable leader

dealer: work as an art dealer

legal: It's legal to drink alcohol at 20.

Script of the Scene

CD: Track 31, 32 / DVD: Chapter 09 (12:08-12:53)

David: You're lying. I know [20](   ) about you. She stole works of art for you. Tell me where she is. You don't want me to come back here with my [21](   ), do you?

Cloutier: Sir, I don't know [22](   ) about ... Olive Green? Me, working with a [23](   )? That's a good one. I'm a respectable art dealer. Everything here is totally [24](   ).

David: But I [25](   ) this information.

Cloutier: Marco!

Comprehension Check

Exercise 1 Who is this man? What does he do?

Name   (   )

Occupation   (   )

Exercise 2 True (T) or false (F)?

1. (   ) David wants to buy a painting.
2. (   ) Cloutier says he doesn't know Olive.
3. (   ) David tries to arrest Cloutier.
4. (   ) David talks to another customer in the shop.

Exercise 3 Answer the following questions.

1. What kind of painting is *Three Village Girls by the Stream*?
   (   )
2. Why is the painting inexpensive?
   (   )
3. Does David think Cloutier knows Olive? Why?
   (   )
4. Who kicked David out of the shop?
   (   )

Grammar

Have / Has to and *must* in positive sentences

→ permission

We have to prepare our presentation by tomorrow.

– Do you have to go home? –Yes, it's already seven. I have to, or my mom will be angry.

I must study English more. I really want to study in the US.

They must leave now, or they'll miss the last train.

＊There is no past tense form for *must*.

○ I had to do my homework yesterday.

✕ I must do my homework yesterday.

Don't have to vs. must not/mustn't

don't have to/doesn't have to

➜ **Something that is not necessary**

You don't have to wash the dishes. Your sister has to do it today.

They don't have to go to the meeting. It's only for the managers.

must not/mustn't

➜ **Something that is prohibited**

They mustn't smoke here. There is a sign.

You mustn't shoot. That's the law.

➜ **Something that should be avoided**

I mustn't drink too much.

You mustn't worry about little things.

Someone, something, etc.

someone something	Someone called me but I was in the shower. I have to tell you something.
anyone anything	You mustn't tell anyone our secret. It was too late. I couldn't do anything.
everyone everything	Everyone at the party is speaking English. Everything in the house is pink or red.
no one nothing	No one in my family likes tomatoes. There was nothing in the box.

*Notes

• *Someone, something*, etc. are used as a singular noun.

• *Someone/something* is usually used in positive sentences and in questions.
• When used in questions, we expect a particular answer.
   Will someone help me? (expecting the answer *Yes*)

• *Anyone/anything* is usually used in questions and in negatives.

Exercise 1 Fill in the blanks with *must* or the correct form of *have to*.

1. Takashi (   ) make a lot of presentations for his business.

2. (   ) I (   ) finish my homework before dinner?

3. Sarah and Meg (   ) go home early last night.

Exercise 2 Fill in the blanks with *mustn't* or *don't / doesn't have to*.

1. It's just between you and me. You (   ) tell anyone.

2. I (   ) wake up early tomorrow, but I normally do.

3. Don't talk so loudly. We (   ) wake up my parents in the next room.

4. I've got a lot of homework. I (   ) go out and play.

Exercise 3 Choose the correct word.

1. (Anyone / Everyone) in school went to Beth's birthday party.

2. There was (anything / nothing) her parents could do to make her happy.

3. We like (everything / something) in this shop. They are all so pretty.

4. I looked for (anyone / someone) for help, but I couldn't find (anyone / someone).

Exercise 4 Reorder the words to make a sentence. The first word is not capitalized.

1. (in / looked / something / strange) this room.

   (   ) this room.

2. There (anyone / in / restaurant / the / wasn't).

   There (   ).

3. (answer / could / no / one) her question.

   (   ) her question.

Speaking Activity

TASK: Giving advice

Your friend, Beth, is coming to Japan for the first time. Read the e-mail from Beth. What advice can you give her? Discuss with your partner(s). Use the **Useful Expressions** to help you.

Step 1: Read the letter from Beth.

Dear [Your Name],

Hi! How have you been? I'm going to visit Japan for the first time with my family. We are going to Okinawa for four nights and five days. We are going in August. I'm very excited, but I'm also worried about many things. Does everyone in Japan speak English? Will it be very hot? My brother and I love scuba diving, so we want to go to Ishigaki Island. Is there anything special we have to do to go to Ishigaki Island? Is there anything else I should know or prepare for? I hope you can help me. Looking forward to hearing from you.

Bye for now,

Beth

Step 2: Think of three things that are necessary to do and two things that are not necessary to do.

Useful Expressions

She should ...	take a dictionary
She must ...	book a ferry
She doesn't have to ...	bring sunscreen
It could/may ...	rent a car for sightseeing
You could/may ...	visit historical sites
There may be ...	arrange a tour package
	get very hot
	get dehydrated
	see tropical fish

Step 3: Write a reply to Beth.

Dear Beth,

Great to hear from you! Here are some tips for you.

I hope you have a great trip!

Sincerely,
[Your name]

CD: Track 33

Listen and fill in the blanks.

A few weeks later, Beth called a travel agent.

Travel agent: Hello, this is Jack from Travel Easy. How may I help you?

Beth: Hi. I saw on ₁ _____ that you have a package tour in English for Japan?

Travel agent: Yes, we do. May I know where you are ₂ _____?

Beth: My family and I are going to ₃ _____ in Okinawa this summer.

Travel agent: How exciting! Are you interested in ₄ _____?

Beth: Very much! My brother and I love ₅ _____.

Travel agent: Great! We have the best tour package for you! Could you tell me

₆ _____ you will be staying in Okinawa?

Beth: ₇ _____ nights.

Travel agent: Okay, then we can arrange a one-day tour package. We can pick your family up at ₈ _____.

At Alfie's Place

The target of this unit is to understand:

・Present perfect vs. past simple（現在完了形と過去形の対比）

・*Can* vs. *could*（canとcouldの対比）

Review Activity

図書館でしなければならないこととしてはならないことをhave toとmustn'tを使って言いましょう。

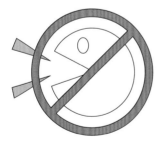

Warm-Up

1. 嘘をつかれたことはありますか？

2. どうしても会いたい人はいますか？

Words and Phrases

CD: Track 34

deal with: deal with the problem

completely: I completely agree with you.

Gosh: Gosh, it's hot today.

clueless: clueless about computers

Who knows?: Emma might become the President. Who knows?

The fact is ...: The fact is... I'm a thief.

scientific: scientific studies

fly: fly to London

number: Can I have your number?

helpful: helpful information for tourists

mate: hang out with a mate

choice: make the right choice

Script of the Scene

CD: Track 35, 36 / DVD: Chapter 10 (12:54-15:05)

David: Look, she's [1]( ) some enemies, and now they are looking for her. I want to find her first and help her deal with the situation.

Alfie: Gosh, you poor boy, you're completely [2]( ), aren't you. Maybe you really wanna help her. [3]( ) [4]( )? But the fact is I haven't [5]( ) her for a long time. She came to London in ... [6]( ), but we couldn't meet up then. I [7]( ) that she spent some time here doing ... scientific research and then [8]( ) [9]( ) to the States.

But that's all I know. Here's my [10]( ). Call me in a few days. I might [11]( ) something [12]( ).

David: Thank you. You've [13]( ) very helpful.

....

David: Look, I just [14]( ) [15]( ) see her. Please, help me, mate.

....

David: I'm not taking this.

Alfie: You don't have much choice if you really want to meet her.

....

Alfie: Good boy.

Exercise 1 What is this key? Who does this key belong to?

(   )

Exercise 2 True (T) or false (F)?

1. (   ) David wants to find Olive.
2. (   ) Alfie told a lie to David.
3. (   ) Alfie gave David his address.
4. (   ) David took the pill.

Exercise 3 Answer the following questions.

1. Who is David looking for?
   (   )
2. Why does David want to help Olive?
   (   )
3. Where does Alfie say Olive is now?
   (   )
4. What did Alfie say Olive was doing in August?
   (   )

Present perfect vs. past simple

Present perfect

➜ **An action or situation that started in the past and continues in the present**

Typical time expressions:

for two days, for a month, this week / month / year, since August, since 2003, recently, lately, yet

Past simple

➜ **An action or situation in the past**

Typical time expressions:

yesterday, last week/month / year, a year ago, three months ago, in 2003, before

Jim has been a waiter in an Italian restaurant for two years.

(Jim became a waiter two years ago and he is still a waiter.)

Jim was a waiter in an Italian restaurant two years ago.

(He is not a waiter anymore.)

I have lived in Tokyo all my life.

(I was born in Tokyo, and I continue to live in Tokyo.)

I lived in Tokyo when I was a university student.

(I am not a student anymore and I am not in Tokyo anymore.)

Can vs. *could*

Can

➜ **For things we <u>are</u> able to do / For things that <u>are</u> possible to do**

Could

➜ **For things we <u>were</u> able to do / For things that <u>were</u> possible to do**

Stephanie can speak Mandarin because she lived in China when she was a child.

– Can I talk to Mr. Johnson? – Sorry, he is busy right now.

We could travel around the world because we won the lottery.

I couldn't eat lunch because I was too busy.

Exercise 1 Complete the sentences with the present perfect or past simple form of the verbs in ( ).

1. I (   ) to Paris when I was 20 years old. (move) I (   ) here for over 6 years now. (live)

2. My parents (   ) in Amsterdam during their business trip. (meet)

3. I have a pet cat named Bell. I (   ) her for ten years. (have)

4. My brother (   ) to the US to study medicine last year. (leave for) He (   ) away for several months. (be) I miss him.

5. Yesterday I (   ) my finger, so I'm going to see the doctor today. (cut)

Exercise 2 Correct the mistakes in the following sentences.

1. We haven't travel for a long time.

   (   )

2. I have finished school last year.

   (   )

3. My daughter has just starts learning English.

   (   )

4. Tom has had his guitar since five years.

   (   )

5. Luckily, I have never breaked an arm or a leg.

   (   )

Exercise 3 Complete the sentences with the verbs in the box with *can, could, can't, couldn't*. You can use each word only once.

solve	see	~~speak~~	wait	hear	write

e.g., *I like travelling a lot. I (**can speak**) many languages.*

1. We had a wonderful room at the hotel. We (   ) the ocean from the window.

2. Sorry, I'll be a bit late. — Don't worry. I've got lots of time. I (   ).

3. I forgot to bring my pen case, so I (   ) anything on my notebook now.

4. I was sitting at the back of the room so I (   ) the lecture very well.

5. His math problems are always difficult. I (   ) any of them when I was in the class.

Speaking Activity

TASK: Choosing a chef

You and your partners are opening a new Japanese restaurant in New York. Talk with the members of your group and decide on a head chef for the kitchen. The head chef must lead a group of Japanese and American chefs.

Step 1: Read the descriptions below about the three candidates.

Name: Paula

Age: 36

Nationality: Spanish

Work experience: She has worked in a Spanish restaurant since she was 22.

Language: Fluent in Spanish. Advanced level in Japanese. Cannot speak English.

Notes: She moved to New York a year ago from Spain.

Name: Takeshi

Age: 42

Nationality: Japanese

Work experience: He was a banker before. He has worked in a Japanese restaurant for two years.

Language: Fluent in Japanese. Intermediate level in English.

Notes: He moved to New York two years ago from Japan.

Name: Antonio

Age: 25

Nationality: Italian

Work experience: He has worked in a Vietnamese restaurant since he was 21.

Language: Fluent in Italian. Intermediate level in English. Beginning level in Japanese.

Notes: He graduated from a cooking school in France. He moved to New York four years ago.

Step 2: **Discuss in your group who should be the head chef. Give your opinions and ask opinions.**

Useful Expressions

(a) Giving opinions and giving reasons
I think (Paula / Takeshi / Antonio) is (not) a good choice because...
(Paula / Takeshi / Antonio) may (not) be a good choice because...
I prefer not to go with (Paula / Takeshi / Antonio) because...

(b) Asking opinions
What do you think?
What about (Paula / Takeshi / Antonio)?
Who should we choose?

(c) Agreeing and disagreeing
I think so too.
I see your point.
I'm not sure about that.

Paula

Takeshi

Antonio

Listen and fill in the blanks.

Jimin: This is a difficult choice. Well, I think $_1$_____ is a good choice because she $_2$_____ in a restaurant for many years.

Daiki: I see your point, but can she $_3$_____ Japanese food? What do you think, Camila?

Camila: I don't think she can. I think $_4$_____ may be a good choice because he $_5$_____ a cooking school. He will be good for the restaurant.

Jimin: I'm not sure about that. He cannot speak $_6$_____ well. What about $_7$_____?

Daiki: Takeshi can speak $_8$_____ and $_9$_____, but he $_{10}$_____ in a restaurant for a long time.

Camila: Okay. Shall we choose between $_{11}$_____ and $_{12}$_____ then?

[Review 1]

1 **Make sentences with the words in ( ). Use *-ing* (gerund) or *to do* (to-infinitive).**

e.g., *Kevin takes photos with his phone.* (+ *like*) → (*Kevin likes to take photos with his phone.*)

1. They drink tea. (+prefer)

→ (   )

2. I ride the train at rush hour. (+not like)

→ (   )

3. My brother plays tennis after school with his friends. (+love)

→ (   )

4. My mother goes out in the summer heat. (+hate)

→ (   )

2 **Complete the sentences with *Why don't we or How about* and the verb in ( ).**

1. A: I don't know the way to the theater.

B: (   ) the police officer over there? (ask)

2. A: I want to go somewhere this weekend.

B: (   ) the art museum in town? (go)

3 **Choose the form which best fits the context.**

1. A: Hey, where are you going? Shopping?

B: Yes. (I'll / I'm going to) buy some presents for my mother's birthday.

2. A: I don't know how to use this app.

B: All right, (I'll / I'm going to) show you.

3. A: What happened to the window?

B: Tom and I broke it. We were playing catch.

A: Mom (will / is going to) be angry.

4. A: Do you want to come to my party this Saturday?

B: Thanks for the invite, but I (will meet / am meeting) my cousin this weekend.

4 **Fill in the blanks with a possessive pronoun.**

1. A: Which car belongs to Mr and Mrs Suzuki?

   B: That one must be (   ). It's parked outside their home.

2. A: May I borrow this pen?

   B: It's not (   ). Mary was sitting on the desk, so it must be

   (   ).

3. A: Is that your car?

   B: No. We parked (   ) near the post office.

5 **Look at the picture. Use *may* or *could*.**

1. What do you think the man will say?   2. What's wrong with the boy?

1. (   ).
2. (   ).

6 **Fill in the blanks with *Shall I* or *Shall we*.**

1. A: (   ) go to the movies tomorrow?

   B: Yes, let's watch an action movie.

2 A: Your bag looks very heavy. (   ) help you?

   B: I'll be okay. Thanks anyway.

3. A: (   ) go now?

   B: Wait a minute. I'm not ready yet.

7 Fill in the blanks with *must not* or *don't/doesn't have to*.

1. They (   ) go to the meeting. It's only for the managers.

2. They (   ) smoke here. There is a sign.

3. Kate (   ) get up early tomorrow. She's having a day off.

8 Fill in the blanks with the words in the box.

something	anything	everything	nothing	someone	anyone

1. Oh no! There's (   ) in the fridge! I'm so hungry.

2. You mustn't tell (   ) our secret.

3. Is there (   ) I can help you with?

4. My parents love cleaning. (   ) in this house is clean.

5. Could you give me (   ) to drink, please?

6. Please wear (   ) formal to the party.

7. I heard (   ) talking in the classroom.

9 Complete the sentences with the present simple, the past simple or present perfect form of the verbs in ( ).

1. According to the time table, the train (   ) at 10:00 on Mondays. (leave)

2. My grandfather (   ) a famous guitarist when he was young. (be)

3. My sister (   ) French for about three years now. (study)

4. My parents (   ) to Italy for their honeymoon ten years ago. (go)

5. I (   ) in Tokyo since my childhood. (live)

6. A: Where are Lisa and Ken?
   B: That's strange. Usually, they (   ) class. (not miss)

10 Complete the sentences with the verbs in the box and *can, could, can't* or *couldn't.* You can use each word only once.

speak	travel	eat	do	answer	swim

1. Stephanie (   ) Mandarin because she was born in China.

2. I broke my arm and (   ) anything last year.

3. I (   ) 10 km when I was young.

4. My boss is very busy right now. She (   ) the phone.

11 Fill in the blanks.

CD: Track 38

Daiki: Hi, Jimin. How ¹(   ) you enjoying your stay in Tokyo?

Jimin: Great! Thank you for taking the time to show me around Tokyo today.

Daiki: No problem. Are you hungry?

Jimin: I'm starving.

Daiki: Okay, ²(   ) don't we go out for lunch first? Do you like ³(   ) eat fresh seafood?

Jimin: Actually, I ⁴(   ) to have meat to fish.

Daiki: No problem. How ⁵(   ) sukiyaki?

Jimin: I ⁶(   ) always wanted to try it.

Daiki: Okay, we ⁷(   ) go to a sukiyaki restaurant then. I know a great place in Ginza.

Jimin: I hear Ginza is expensive ....

Daiki: It ⁸(   ) be a bit expensive. But don't worry. It's on me!

Jimin: Oh, Daiki. You ⁹(   ) have ¹⁰(   ) pay for me.

Daiki: Really, I want to. You ¹¹(   ) all the way to Japan.

Jimin: Thank you!

[Unit 7]

David in a Trap

The target of this unit is to understand:

・State verbs with present continuous forms（現在進行形の状態動詞）

・Countable and uncountable nouns（可算名詞と不可算名詞）

・*How many ...?* or *How much ...?*（How many ...? や How much ...? を含む文）

Review Activity

ペアを組み、以前はできたのに今はできなくなってしまったこと、また、以前はできなかったのに今はできるようになったことを英語で話し合いましょう。

Warm-Up

1. 徹夜したことはありますか？

2. どんな人に好感を持ちますか？

Scene 7

Words and Phrases

CD (Disc 2): Track 01

have second thoughts: He's having second thoughts about going abroad.

instead:
There's no meat! Then I'll take fish instead.

be ahead of: Carry is ahead of Jim in the race.

biscuit: give some biscuits to pigeons

share: share a dish with friends

rational: rational behavior

cop: A cop will find you.

pain in the arse: This work is a pain in the arse.

be jealous of: I am jealous of her talent.

clearly: It was clearly a mistake.

have a soft spot for: I have a soft spot for animals, especially rabbits.

moron: a moron like him

be emotional about:
He is emotional about the past.

feeling: think about other people's feelings

weak point: Jim's weak point is his pride.

loo: a public loo

hide: hide a treasure box

be obsessed: You're obsessed with your smartphone.

guy: What's up, guys?

turn around: Turn around! There's a car behind you!

not quite: The work is not quite finished.

Script of the Scene

CD (Disc 2): Track 02, 03 / DVD: Chapter 11 (15:06-16:48)

Alfie: I'm ^{1}( ) second thoughts about tea. Let's have some ^{2}( ) instead, huh? There is a long night ahead of us.

Olive: You're not ^{3}( ) him.

Alfie: Yes, I am. I may have ^{4}( ) ^{5}( ) biscuits, but I'm not sharing because they are my favourite. Be ^{6}( ). He's a cop and a pain in the arse. He knows ^{7}( ) ^{8}( ) about you and me. Also, I'm ^{9}( ) of him. You clearly have a soft spot for that moron.

Olive: I do not have a soft spot for him or ^{10}( ) ^{11}( ). He may be a moron, but you ^{12}( ) kill him.

Alfie: Why? You're ^{13}( ) too emotional about this. ^{14}( ) are one of women's weak points.

Olive: Alfie, no.

Alfie: That's my ^{15}( ). Where did you find it?

Olive: In the ^{16}( ). There are guns hidden all over this place. You're ^{17}( ).

David: Guys, [18](   ) [19](   )!

Alfie: It's [20](   ) one man. We can deal with that, can't we, luv?

Cloutier: Not quite, mes amis. Not quite.

Comprehension Check

Exercise 1 Who are Alfie and Olive pointing their guns at?

Exercise 2 True (T) or false (F)?

1. (   ) Both Alfie and Olive try to kill David.

2. (   ) David escapes from Alfie and runs away.

3. (   ) Alfie thinks Olive likes David.

4. (   ) Olive found a knife in the kitchen.

Exercise 3 Answer the following questions.

1. Why does Alfie want to kill David?

(   )

2. Why is Alfie jealous of David?

(   )

3. What does Alfie say is a woman's weak point?

(   )

4. Who showed up in the end?

(   )

5. Where did Olive find a gun?

(   )

Grammar

State verbs with present continuous forms

Some state verbs can be used in present continuous, but their meaning changes.

being/existing: *be*-verb, *remain, resemble, live, exist, stay*
feeling: *like, love, hate, want, enjoy*
possessing: *have, own, belong to*
thinking: *believe, understand*
sensing: *feel, hear, taste, see, listen to, smell*

My students are quiet. (generally)
My students are being quiet today. (temporary behavior)

I don't enjoy parties because it's loud. (generally)
I'm enjoying this party because there aren't too many people. (temporary behavior)

Countable and uncountable nouns

Countable nouns	Uncountable nouns
→ things that can be individually counted	→ things that cannot be divided into separate elements
a bottle, a chair, a candle, a plate	music, soup, water, bread, butter, meat, wine, bread, information, money/cash, water
How many eggs are there? – There are two eggs. – There are many eggs. – There aren't many eggs.	How much rice is there? – There is some rice. – There is so much rice. – There isn't much rice.
a banana / two burgers / some eggs / a few desks / many books / a lot of houses / lots of cans	some rice (a rice) / a little juice / much water / a lot of wine / lots of money a bag of → a bag of sugar, a bag of rice a glass of → a glass of water, a glass of beer a bottle of → a bottle of wine, a bottle of soda a piece of → a piece of information, a piece of bread

Exercise 1 Circle the items that are countable in the box below.

cup	milk	love	beef
egg	laptop	information	dream
paper	glass	student	advice
butter	soup	bread	ice

Exercise 2 Make questions with *how much* or *how many*. Then write your answers to the questions.

e.g., *How many* steps do you walk every day?

Answer (*I walk about ten thousand steps every day.*)

1. _____ hours of sleep do you have every night?

   Answer (   )

2. _____ water do you drink every day?

   Answer (   )

3. _____ students are in your class?

   Answer (   )

4. _____ time do you spend on your phone every day?

   Answer (   )

Exercise 3 Correct the mistakes in the following sentences.

1. My father and I went to nice restaurant yesterday.

   (   )

2. There were a lot of kid in the park.

   (   )

3. How much children do you have?

   (   )

4. We have done many research on the topic.

   (   )

Speaking Activity

TASK: Coming up with a recipe

You and your partners must cook a dish that is delicious but cheap. Choose one dish from the following: fried rice, curry and rice, pancakes, hamburgers, omelets. The dish must be for four people. You must use <u>three ingredients</u>.

Step 1: Label the following items.

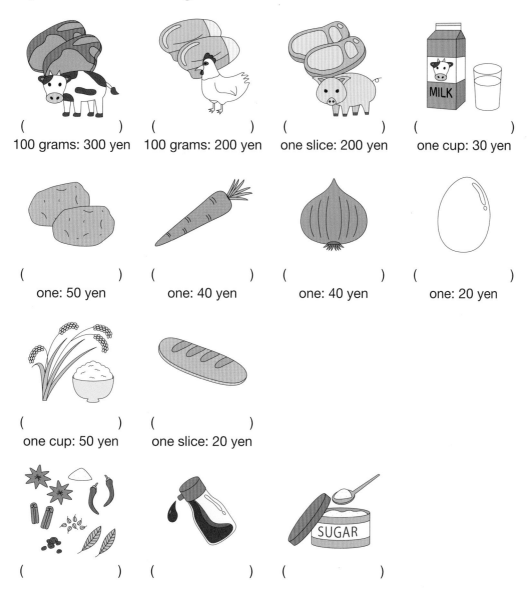

(   )   (   )   (   )   (   )

100 grams: 300 yen   100 grams: 200 yen   one slice: 200 yen   one cup: 30 yen

(   )   (   )   (   )   (   )

one: 50 yen   one: 40 yen   one: 40 yen   one: 20 yen

(   )   (   )

one cup: 50 yen   one slice: 20 yen

(   )   (   )   (   )

one tablespoon: 10 yen each

Step 2: In your group, choose <u>three ingredients</u> from Step 1 to decide on a dish.

Useful Expressions

(a) Making suggestions

How about ...?

I think we should make ....

We can make a lot of food with ...

(b) Asking for information and answering

How many ... do we need?

How much ... do we need?

How much does it cost?

We need ... grams of ...

A tablespoon of ... costs ...

A piece of ... costs ...

Step 3: What did your group decide? What do you need to make the dish?

Dish: _____

Ingredients

(1)

(2)

(3)

CD (Disc 2): Track 04

Listen and fill in the blanks.

Daiki: I love spaghetti. How about some spaghetti?

Jimin: I don't think so, Daiki. We can't make pasta. It's not on the list.

Jimin: I think we should make 1 _____. We don't need many

2 _____.

Daniel: Okay, what do we need?

Daiki: I can tell you. I always make fried rice. We need some 3 _____, rice,

4 _____, eggs, and 5 _____.

Daniel: 6 _____ is expensive.

Jimin: We don't have to put 7 _____. We can make 8 _____ fried

rice.

Daiki: Good idea!

Daniel: How much 9 _____ do we need?

Daiki: We need 10 _____ of rice for four people. How much does it cost?

Jimin: It's only 11 _____. How many 12 _____?

Unit 8

Confrontation

The target of this unit is to understand:

・Past continuous（過去進行形を含む文）
・Using past continuous and past simple together (*when*, *while*)（過去進行形と過去形が共に使われる文）

Review Activity

次の絵の現在の状況を説明してみましょう。

She is usually kind, but right now ...

The dog is usually noisy, but right now ...

Warm-Up

1. 人に裏切られたことはありますか？
2. 100万円があったら、どんなことに使いますか？

Let's Watch!

Scene 8

 **Words and Phrases**

◀))) CD (Disc 2): Track 05

business partner: start a company with
  business partners

ungrateful: It's ungrateful of you to say that.

introduce: Let me introduce myself.

invest:
  invest much money to open a restaurant

fortune: pay a fortune for a car

pay back: Pay me back as soon as possible.

pay peanuts:
  I got paid peanuts for hard work.

betray:
  I can't believe you betrayed your husband!

nearly:
  It costs nearly one hundred million yen.

two-faced: a two-faced liar

fraud: The fraud sold a fake painting.

Come on!: Come on! I'm only joking!

good old: the good old days

a couple of:
  I will be ready in a couple of minutes.

friendship: have a good friendship with
  the neighbors

die: My grandfather died from old age.

Script of the Scene   ◀))) CD (Disc 2): Track 06, 07 / DVD: Chapter 12 (16:49-19:22)

Olive: How did you know where I am?

Cloutier: Marco ¹(   ) ²(   ) your friend around all day.

Alfie: I told you he was a moron. Who are they?

Olive: Alfie, meet Mr Cloutier, an ³(   ) ⁴(   ). He was my
            business partner a couple of years ago.

Cloutier: A ⁵(   ) ⁶(   )? You ungrateful girl. I taught you
            everything you know about ⁷(   ) art. I introduced you to my
            ⁸(   ). I invested a fortune in you.

Olive: I paid it all back. For years, I ⁹(   ) ¹⁰(   ) for you, and
            you ¹¹(   ) ¹²(   ) me peanuts. I made you a rich man.

Cloutier: Then you betrayed me. You took nearly all my clients. And I'm here to kill you
            for that.

Olive: Good luck, you ¹³(   ) fraud.

Cloutier: Alfie? [14](   ) I [15](   ) you Alfie? In my car, there's a suitcase with [16](   ) pounds in it. It can be [17](   ). But you have to help me kill Olive and her friend.

Olive: Come on, Alfie. I'll get you [18](   ) [19](   ) money in a couple of days.

Cloutier: Maybe she will or maybe [20](   ) [21](   ). But I've got cash. Lots of [22](   ) [23](   ) cash that I can give you now.

Olive: Alfie, don't listen to him. Think about our [24](   ) friendship.

Alfie: The answer is "no". I can kill him, but not Olive.

Cloutier: I understand. But, Alfie, [25](   ) [26](   ). There are people following her. People who know [27](   ) you are and [28](   ) you do. You must understand that Olive's a problem now. You don't want to lose all this.

Alfie: The man's right. I'm sorry, Olive, our special friendship is [29](   ). Drop the gun or he dies.

Comprehension Check

Exercise 1 What was the relationship between Olive and Cloutier?

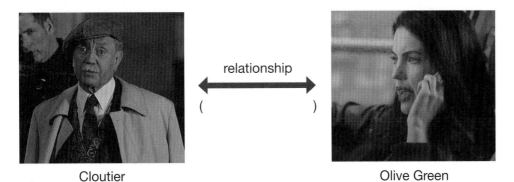

relationship

(   )

Cloutier   Olive Green

Exercise 2 True (T) or false (F)?

1. (   ) Cloutier gave her a high salary in the past.
2. (   ) Marco helped Cloutier find Olive.
3. (   ) Cloutier can pay Alfie with a check.
4. (   ) Alfie changed his mind.

Exercise 3 Answer the following questions.

1. What did Cloutier teach Olive in the past?

   (   )

2. Why is Cloutier angry at Olive?

   (   )

3. How much money can Cloutier give Alfie?

   (   )

4. In the end, why does Alfie agree with Cloutier?

   (   )

Past continuous

→ **An action or event that was in progress at some time in the past**

My parents and I were watching TV at home. My favorite band was playing in a music program.

– I went to your office yesterday at 1 pm, but I couldn't find you. Were you meeting with your client?
– I wasn't meeting with my clients, but I was having lunch with my colleagues then.

Using past continuous and past simple together (*when, while*)

→ **The past continuous describes a longer action; the past simple describes a shorter action.**

My brother came in **while my mother and I were talking**.
= **While my mother and I were talking**, my brother came in.

Mary was sleeping **when the phone rang**.
= **When the phone rang**, Mary was sleeping.

Exercise 1 Reorder the words to make a sentence.

1. I (for / studying / test / the / was) until midnight.

   I (   ) until midnight.

2. What (doing / in / library / the / were / you)?

   What (   )?

3. Jim (listening / teacher / the / to / wasn't) in the class.

   Jim (   ) in the class.

4. When I woke up, (my / news / parents / the / watching / were).

   When I woke up, (   ).

Exercise 2 Fill in the blanks with the past simple or past continuous form of the verbs in ( ).

1. I _____ (do) my homework when my brother _____ (come) home.

2. It _____ (start) to rain while the students _____ (eat) lunch.

3. While Jessica _____ (prepare) breakfast, her children _____ (wake up).

4. When their mother _____ (get) home, the children _____ (play) video games.

Exercise 3 Complete the story with the past simple or past continuous form of the verbs in ( ).

Last year when I $_1$_____ (have) lunch with my friend at a café, we $_2$_____ (hear) a loud noise. Soon after, something $_3$_____ (flash) in the sky for a few seconds. It couldn't be lightening because it $_4$_____ (not rain). Some people $_5$_____ (think) that it was a UFO, but I didn't think so. I mean, really? A UFO ...?

Speaking Activity

TASK: Telling a story

With a partner, you will take turns talking about an event that happened to you in the past. It could be something unbelievable, wonderful, exciting, terrible, or frightening.

Step 1: Prepare what you want to talk about. Answer the following questions.

1. Where were you when this event happened?
   (   )
2. When did it happen?
   (   )
3. Who were you with?
   (   )
4. How did you react?
   (   )
5. How were people reacting when this happened?
   (   )
6. How did it end?
   (   )

Useful Expressions

Feelings

I was ...
     scared / happy / excited / surprised / sad / disappointed / angry / frustrated / bored / frightened
It was ...
     funny / interesting / strange / scary / sad / exciting / shocking / frightening

Reactions
I screamed, ran away, laughed, called the police.   I was crying, panicking, yelling, hiding, jumping up and down

Step 2: Tell your story to your partner.

🔊 CD (Disc 2): Track **08**

Listen and fill in the blanks.

Jimin: Daiki, tell me about an incredible thing that happened to you.

Daiki: Okay, it's very ₁ _____. Are you ready?

Jimin: Ohhh. I love scary stories.

Daiki: I was six years old. I ₂ _____ TV with my brother when we

₃ _____ a big noise. My brother ₄ _____ upstairs.

I ₅ _____ in the bathroom when my brother ₆ _____.

I ₇ _____ upstairs. I ₈ _____ my brother in our bedroom.

And a bat ₉ _____!

Jimin: Oh my gosh! What happened?

Daiki: We ₁₀ _____ for our mom! We were so frightened.

Digging a Grave

The target of this unit is to understand:

・Passive voice: *be* + past participle （受動態を含む文）

Review Activity

ペアを組み、昨晩、何をしていたのかを過去進行形を使って話し合いましょう。

e.g., *A: What were you doing at 10 in the morning?*
   B: I was riding a train.

10 AM	
12 PM	
4 PM	
8 PM	
12 AM	

Warm-Up

1. 何かやめたい癖や習慣はありますか？
2. 落ち着きたいとき、何をしますか？

Let's Watch!

Scene 9-1

Words and Phrases

CD (Disc 2): Track 09

grateful: I'm grateful for the job offer.

hard: a hard question

bury: The dog buried a bone in the garden.

popular: a popular boy band

grave: visit my great grandparents' grave

dig: dig a hole

proper: wear proper clothes for the party

depth: measure the depth of the sea

foot: How long is ten feet in centimeters?

shallow: a shallow part of the lake

resident: foreign residents in Japan

wild animal: protect wild animals

basically: I basically agree with you.

quit ... ing: quit drinking

smoke: You can't smoke here.

Script of the Scene

CD (Disc 2): Track 10, 11 / DVD: Chapter 13 (19:23-20:34)

Alfie: So grateful for the jacket, David. You know, it's hard these days to find a ¹( ) ²( ) ³( ) burying bodies in England. This one's quite popular. ⁴( ) ⁵( ) have been dug here. But most of them have been ⁶( ) ⁷( ) that one. Look, a proper grave is dug to a depth of five feet or more. If it is too shallow, then the body is usually ⁸( ) ⁹( ) the police, or local residents, or even wild animals.

Cloutier: Are they ready?

Alfie: Yeah ... ¹⁰( ) ¹¹( ).

Cloutier: Damn! I can't do it. I don't do this ¹²( ) ¹³( ), okay? Just give me ¹⁴( ) ¹⁵( ) alone.

Alfie: Wait. I've ¹⁶( ) quit smoking, but I could have one.

Words and Phrases

With pleasure: Will you help me?—With pleasure.

Script of the Scene

CD (Disc 2): Track 13, 14 / DVD: Chapter 14 (20:35-21:29)

Olive: David, ¹⁷(   ) ¹⁸(   ).

....

Olive: David, now!

David: With ¹⁹(   ).

Comprehension Check

Exercise 1 What are David and Olive doing?

Exercise 2 True (T) or false (F)?

1. (   ) Alfie likes David's jacket.
2. (   ) It's easy to find places for burying bodies in England.
3. (   ) A proper grave must be at least three feet deep.
4. (   ) Alfie doesn't smoke anymore.

Exercise 3 **Answer the following questions.**

1. Why are Olive and David digging a hole?

   (   )

2. According to Alfie, how deep should a grave be?

   (   )

3. What did Olive do to Marco?

   (   )

4. What happens if a grave is shallow?

   (   )

5. Why was Cloutier nervous?

   (   )

Grammar

Passive voice: *be* + past participle

➡ the performer of the action is known / important (in this case, *by* + performer)

· *Present simple*

My father usually cooks dinner on weekends.

➡ Dinner is usually cooked by my father on weekends.

· *Past simple*

My friend wrote this beautiful song. ➡ This beautiful song was written by my friend.

· *Present perfect*

Pierre has asked me out on a date. ➡ I have been asked out on a date by Pierre.

➡the performer of the action is unknown / unimportant (in this case, ~~by + performer~~)

· *Present simple*

Somebody cleans the park in my town every day.

➡ The park in my town is cleaned every day.

· *Past simple*

People called me Beth at school. ➡ I was called Beth at school.

· *Present perfect*

Somebody has broken the school window. ➡ The school window has been broken.

Exercise 1 **Reorder the words to make a sentence.**

1. Michael (by / is / liked / many / people).

   Michael (   ).

2. Your (been / has / meal / paid for) already.

   Your (   ) already.

3. My (children / invited / the / to / weren't) party.

   My (   ) party.

Exercise 2   **Change the following sentences into the passive voice.**

1. My mother cleaned my room.

   → (   )

2. Many fans support this team.

   → (   )

3. Rick has completed the jigsaw puzzle.

   → (   )

4. People call my little sister Pipi.

   → (   )

Exercise 3   **Choose the correct form.**

1. While I was in Old Berry, my watch (stole / was stolen) from my hotel room.

2. The police officer (reported / was reported) the accident immediately.

3. It is a big company. A thousand people (employed / are employed) there.

4. Mr. Tanaka was born in Japan but (grew up / was grown up) in the U.S.

Speaking Activity

TASK: Talking about famous paintings

With a partner, take turns talking about famous paintings. In the end, find a painting you like and tell your partner about it.

Step 1: Read the information about *The Starry Night* and the *Mona Lisa*.

Van Gogh painted *The Starry Night*.

His birthplace is the Netherlands.

He painted it in France.

He painted it in June 1889.

The Museum of Modern Art (MoMA) in New York has *The Starry Night*.

Leonardo da Vinci painted the *Mona Lisa.*

His birthplace is Italy.

He painted it between 1506 and 1507.

He painted it in Florence.

The Louvre in France has the *Mona Lisa*.

Step 2: Tell your partner about *The Starry Night* or the *Mona Lisa* with the passive voice. Use the information in Step 1.

Step 3: Talk about a painting that you know. Use the passive voice.

1. Who was it painted by?
   (   )
2. Where was the artist born?
   (   )
3. When was it painted?
   (   )
4. Where is the painting located?
   (   )

Thirty-six Views of Mt. Fuji
by Hokusai

Water Lilies
by Monet

Girl with a Pearl Earring
by Vermeer

The Last Supper by da Vinci

🔊 CD (Disc 2): **Track 15**

Listen and fill in the blanks.

Daiki: Jimin, do you know about René Magritte?

Jimin: No. Who is he?

Daiki: He was a very famous painter. He was born in 1_____. A very famous
picture, *The Son of Man*, was painted by 2_____. This was painted in
3_____. It is known as 4_____.

Jimin: That's very interesting. Where can I see it?

Daiki: I think the painting can 5_____ in the San Francisco Museum of
Modern Art, but I'm not sure.

Another Confrontation

The target of this unit is to understand:

・Adverbs（副詞）

・Comparatives (adverbs)（比較を含む文）

・Superlatives (adverbs)（最上級を含む文）

Review Activity

次の表の建物について、例のように受動態を使って説明しましょう。

e.g. *The Leaning Tower of Pisa was built by Bonanno Pisano.*

	Leaning Tower of Pisa	Palace and Park of Versailles
Where	Pisa, Italy	Yvelines, France
When	1372	1682
Who	Bonanno Pisano	Louis XIV
		Yvelines / iːvlíːn /

Warm-Up

1. 今では慣れたことで、初めは緊張したことは何ですか？
2. 危機から脱した経験はありますか？

Words and Phrases

🔊 CD (Disc 2): Track 16

for the first time: I visited New York for the first time last year.

like (preposition): Listening with these speakers is like going to a concert.

do a parachute jump:
   try to do a parachute jump

hardly: I could hardly sleep yesterday.

give ... a thought: You want to change jobs? You should give it a thought.

exactly: What's that exactly?

Armed Forces: join the Armed Forces

Special Air Service: a training in the Special Air Service

be out of one's mind: She must be out of her mind to do such a thing.

behave: The children behaved well.

badly: He sings badly.

That's true:
   That's true. You're completely right.

no hard feelings: He had no hard feelings against me.

None whatsoever!: You have no idea what I am saying? – None whatsoever!

Script of the Scene

🔊 CD (Disc 2): Track 17, 18 / DVD: Chapter 15 (21:30-23:18)

Alfie: You know, shooting a man for the first time is like doing a parachute jump. After the first time, you [1](   ) give it a thought.

Cloutier: How many [2](   ) have you killed, exactly?

Alfie: That's a big question. Most of them I killed when I was in the Armed Forces. The [3](   ) Special Air Service. We were [4](   ) [5](   ). I loved that job.

Cloutier: Did you hear that?

Olive: Alfie, [6](   ) him the gun.

Alfie: Are you out of your [7](   )? You shot at me? I'm your bloody [8](   ) [9](   )!

   ....

Alfie: David, wow. That was as good as mine. But I want you to know this. I behaved [10](   ) towards you, that's true. But it's only because Olive clearly likes you [11](   ) [12](   ) me. So, no hard feelings, yeah?

David: None [13](   ).

Alfie: Really? Oh shit!

Comprehension Check

Exercise 1 Olive has one gun on Cloutier. Who is she pointing the other gun at?

Exercise 2 True (T) or false (F)?

1. (   ) Cloutier has never murdered anyone.
2. (   ) Alfie has murdered many people in his career.
3. (   ) Alfie served in the Marine Corps.
4. (   ) David apologized to Alfie.

Exercise 3 Answer the following questions.

1. According to Alfie, what is like doing a parachute jump?
   (   )
2. Which armed forces did Alfie belong to?
   (   )
3. Why did Alfie get upset at Olive?
   (   )
4. Why does Alfie say he behaved badly toward David?
   (   )

Adverbs

adjective + *ly*

beautifully: The opera singer sang beautifully.

slowly: A turtle walks slowly.

the same as the adjective

fast: He runs fast.

high: A kangaroo jumps high.

different from the adjective

well: They speak French well.

Comparatives (adverbs)

***more* + adverb**

more beautifully: The opera singer sang more beautifully than the other singer.

more slowly: A turtle walks more slowly than a duck.

adverb + *er*

faster: He runs faster than his teacher.

higher: A kangaroo jumps higher than a frog.

irregular

well → better: They speak French better than last year.

Superlatives (adverbs)

superlatives: *the most* + adverb

the most carefully: The opera singer sang the most beautifully in the group.

the most slowly: Among ducks, rabbits, and turtles, turtles walk the most slowly.

the* + adverb + *est

the fastest: He runs the fastest in the family.

the highest: Kangaroos jump the highest in the zoo.

irregular

well → the best: They speak French the best in their class.

∗ Notes

These adverbs can also take the ending -ly, but the meaning changes.

hard = difficult or tough

hardly = very little, almost nothing: I hardly know you.

near = close

nearly = almost: I nearly believed you.

late = happening after the expected time

lately = in the last days / weeks: I've been very busy lately.

Exercise 1 Write the comparative and superlative form of the following adverbs.

	Comparative	Superlative
1. slowly	( )	( )
2. fast	( )	( )
3. beautifully	( )	( )
4. well	( )	( )

Exercise 2 Choose the correct word.

1. The people were (bad / badly) injured in the accident.
2. Susan has the flu and has (hard / hardly) eaten anything for a few days.
3. Life is short. Time passes so (quick / quickly).
4. My dog can jump very (high / highly). It's amazing.
5. Please don't come home so (late / lately).
6. I was gambling in Las Vegas and (near / nearly) lost all of my money.

Exercise 3 Complete the sentences with the comparative or superlative form of the adverbs in ( ).

1. My team lost the soccer match. We have to practice ( ). (hard)
2. I have three brothers. The oldest runs ( ). (fast)
3. Which can move ( ): A cheetah or a bullet train? (quickly)
4. There is no one that can cook ( ) than my mom. (well)

Exercise 4 Correct the mistakes in the following sentences.

1. My neighbor's dog runs more fastly than mine.

   (   )

2. Sarah answered the questions more better than her classmates.

   (   )

3. The Italian restaurant is the most deliciously in my town.

   (   )

4. She lives happilier now because she has a new job.

   (   )

Speaking Activity

TASK: Comparing party venues

You and your peers are going to throw a birthday party for a friend. The party will be for 20 people. Compare the different venues and decide on the best one for the party.

Step 1: You can choose from four options. In your group, think of advantages and disadvantages of the following options.

Picnic in a rose garden

Advantage:	It will be nice on a sunny day. It is outside and you don't have to worry about noise.
Disadvantage:	It will be terrible on a rainy day. You have to clean up.

Birthday at an amusement park

Advantage:	It will be fun! There are many things to do.
Disadvantage:	The location may not be convenient. It will be expensive.

Dinner at a hotel restaurant

Advantage: You will have wonderful food.

                    You have to be careful with noise.

Disadvantage: It may be expensive.

                    Some people may not like the food.

Home party

Advantage: It will be cheap

                    It will be relaxing.

Disadvantage: The neighbors could get angry.

                    You have to work hard to prepare.

Step 2: **Look at your notes and discuss. Where will you have the birthday party?**

Useful Expressions

(a) Making suggestions
How about ...?
I think we should have a party at ...
Why don't we have a party at ...?
Shall we have a party at ...?
We should have a party at ...

(b) Comparing
... will be more fun than ...
... will cost more than ...
People can go to ... more easily than ...
People can relax more at ... than at ...
People can talk more loudly at ... than at ...
The food will taste better at ... than at ...
People will have to travel the farthest.
You have to work the hardest for ...
... will cost the most.

(c) Agreeing and disagreeing

I completely agree!

That's exactly what I was thinking!

I know what you mean but ...

I see your point but ...

I think so too but ...

CD (Disc 2): Track **19**

Listen and fill in the blanks.

Jimin: Where should we hold the birthday party?

Daiki: Well, I think we should have the party at ₁_____.

Camila: Yeah, that's exactly what I was thinking. It'll be ₂_____.

Jimin: I think so too, but it will ₃_____ the other places. What about

₄_____?

Daiki: Hotel restaurants are also expensive... A home party will

₅_____ a restaurant.

Camila: I agree. We have to invite 20 people. People will not be able to

₆_____ relax.

Daiki: Okay, then we should have a party outside. ₇_____! It'll be

₈_____ and people can talk ₉_____ outside than

inside.

Jimin: That's a good idea. What if it rains?

Daiki: Well, let's just keep our fingers crossed!

Great, Now We're Trapped

The target of this unit is to understand:

・Question tags（付加疑問文）
・*Wh*-question words (*who, what, when, where*)（wh疑問文）

Review Activity

ペアを組み、次の質問に答えましょう。

・Who sings more beautifully, you or your mother?
・Who cooks the best in your family?
・Which animals walk more slowly, dogs or cats?
・Which animals jump the highest?
・Which transportation moves the most quickly?

Warm-Up

1. キャンプをするとき、何が必要ですか？
2. 安物を買って損をした経験はありますか？

Words and Phrases

CD (Disc 2): Track 20

pretty: I'm pretty well. Thank you.

solid: a solid foundation

organise (organize): organise the party

and stuff: Can you bring food and stuff to the party?

starve: When's dinner? I'm starving.

freeze to death: Many animals froze to death last winter.

business is slow: We haven't been successful because business has been slow.

recently: This has been in fashion recently.

You're joking.: There's no cake for me? You're joking, right?

on the other hand: My sister is loud. On the other hand, I'm very quiet.

actually: She's actually a thief.

respect: show respect for her

wallet: a stolen wallet

Script of the Scene

CD (Disc 2): **Track 21, 22** / DVD: **Chapter 16** (23:19-24:35)

Olive: Good. OK, guys, that looks pretty solid, [1]( ) [2]( )? Now, we need to organise some food and stuff for you. We can't let you starve or freeze to death here, [3]( ) [4]( )? Now, about the money.

David: There is still 50k in Cloutier's [5]( ). I can go and ...

Alfie: [6]( ) [7]( ) no money in your car, is there?

Cloutier: What? Business has been slow recently. I really wanted to pay you. 1,000 pounds or so.

Alfie: 1,000 quid? You're [8]( ), right? But on the other hand, a grand is not actually bad for four hours' work, [9]( ) [10]( )?

Olive: I'm losing the little respect I had for you, Alfie. Now, [11]( ) did you put my wallet?

Alfie: It's in my shop, in [12]( ). Together with his.

 **Words and Phrases**

sleeping bag: sleep in a sleeping bag

compact: buy a light, compact laptop

water-proof: a water-proof bag

space blanket: a space blanket for thermal protection

keep ... warm: keep the room warm

in all weathers: Professional athletes must play in all weathers.

afford: I can afford this house.

Script of the Scene   CD (Disc 2): Track 24, 25 / DVD: Chapter 17 (24:36-25:37)

David: Sleeping bag, compact, water-proof, [13](   ) pounds. No way.
[14](   ) [15](   ) ... keeps you warm in all weathers ...
[16](   ) pounds. All right. A [17](   ) ... 1 pound 50.
Will one be enough? Damn it! Toilet paper ... regular or [18](   )
[19](   )? Regular is only 99p. Sorry guys.

....

David: I need some sandwiches. But I [20](   ) really [21](   )
them, so ...

Words and Phrases

feed: Don't feed wild animals

free of charge: This concert is free of charge.

stale: stale bread

get rid of: get rid of old clothes

Script of the Scene   CD (Disc 2): Track 27, 28 / DVD: Chapter 18 (25:38-25:51)

David: Please, I need to [22](   ) my friends. If I don't bring them any food ...

Shop Assistant: You can have all the sandwiches [23](   ) [24](   )
[25](   ). They are stale and I need to get rid of them anyway.
Yeah, take them all. And [26](   ) [27](   ).

Comprehension Check

Exercise 1 Where does she work?

Exercise 2 True (T) or false (F)?

1. (　　　) There is 50K in Cloutier's car.
2. (　　　) A space blanket was more expensive than a sleeping bag.
3. (　　　) David chose extra soft toilet paper.
4. (　　　) David got the sandwiches for free.

Exercise 3 Answer the following questions.

1. Where is Olive's wallet?
   (　　　　　　　　　　　　　　　　　　　　　　　　　　　　　　）
2. Why did David choose a space blanket over a sleeping bag?
   (　　　　　　　　　　　　　　　　　　　　　　　　　　　　　　）
3. How much was the bucket?
   (　　　　　　　　　　　　　　　　　　　　　　　　　　　　　　）
4. Why did the shop assistant give the sandwiches free of charge?
   (　　　　　　　　　　　　　　　　　　　　　　　　　　　　　　）

Grammar

Question tags

positive statement, <u>negative tag</u>?
negative statement, <u>positive tag</u>?

be-simple	I am sick, <u>aren't I</u>?
be-past	He wasn't here, <u>was he</u>?
do-simple	You washed the dishes, <u>didn't you</u>?
do-past	She didn't come to school, <u>did she</u>?
perfect-*have*	It has rained, <u>hasn't it</u>?
can	We can't swim here, <u>can we</u>?
will	They'll have a meeting, <u>won't they</u>?
there	There's nothing in the fridge, <u>is there</u>?

Wh-question words (*who, what, when, where*)

	<u>**Ben** played **baseball** **in the park** **yesterday**</u>.
who (person):	<u>Who</u> played baseball in the park yesterday?
what (object):	<u>What</u> did Ben play in the park yesterday?
when (time):	<u>When</u> did Ben play baseball in the park?
where (place):	<u>Where</u> did Ben play baseball yesterday?

Exercise 1 Add a question tag to the following sentences.

1. Sarah came to work early this morning, ( )?
2. You'll be late for dinner again tonight, ( )?
3. Bob can sing better than Carol, ( )?
4. There's some food in the fridge, ( )?
5. This winter hasn't been cold, ( )?
6. They won't get us in trouble, ( )?

Exercise 2 Fill in the blanks with an appropriate *wh*-question word.

1. A: (   ) did you go to Hawaii?

   B: I went there last year with my family.

2. A: (   ) cooked this food? It's delicious!

   B: I did! I'm glad you like it.

3. A: (   ) did my dog go?

   B: Over there. I think he's headed to the park.

4. A: (   ) did you get for Katy for her birthday?

   B: I got her a beautiful red purse. I hope she likes it!

Exercise 3 Make *wh*-questions for the following dialogues. The questions should ask for the <u>underlined</u> information.

e.g., *A: (What did he buy at the store?)*

   B: He bought <u>a book</u> at the store.

1. A: (   )

   B: <u>Banksy</u> is the best artist in my opinion.

2. A: (   )

   B: I like to <u>play the piano</u> in my free time.

3. A: (   )

   B: I want to go <u>to Thailand</u> this summer.

4. A: (   )

   B: The restaurant opens <u>at 11 o'clock</u>.

Speaking Activity

TASK: You know your partner very well, don't you?

Let's see how well you know your partner. Ask about your partner and check how well you remember about him/her.

Step 1: First, ask and answer each other the following questions. <u>Do not take any notes</u>!

1. When is your birthday?
2. Where were you born?
3. Do you have any brothers or sisters?
4. What kind of food do you not like?
5. Can you play a musical instrument?
6. What do you like to do in your free time?
7. What will you do this weekend?
8. What is the most exciting place you have been to?

Step 2: Now check how much you know about your partner by using question tags. How much could you remember about your partner? Keep a score.

	☺	☹
1.		
2.		
3.		
4.		
5.		
6.		
7.		
8.		

Listen and fill in the blanks.

Daiki: Jimin, can I ask you some questions?

Jimin: Sure, go ahead.

Daiki: When is your birthday?

Jimin: It's $_1$_____.

Daiki: Where were you born?

Jimin: I was born in $_2$_____.

Daiki: That's really nice. Do you have any brothers or sisters?

Jimin: Yes, I have two $_3$_____.

Daiki: Okay. What kind of food do you not like?

Jimin: Hmm ... let me see. I don't like $_4$_____!

....

Daiki: Okay, let me see how much I remember. Your birthday is on April 20th,

$_5$_____?

Jimin: Wow, good memory, Daiki! That's right

Daiki: And you were born in Okinawa, $_6$_____?

Jimin: Correct again!

Daiki: You have two siblings ... You have two brothers, $_7$_____?

Jimin: Oh no. That's incorrect. I have two sisters.

Daiki: Oh, I'm sorry. Okay. Next. You don't like spicy foods, $_8$_____?

Jimin: That's right.

[Unit **12**]

It's Up to You, David

The target of this unit is to understand:

・Relative clauses (*who, whom, which, where, when*)（関係節を含む文）
・*When* + present simple, present continuous（whenを含む文）

Review Activity

それぞれの写真について尋ねる英文を作りましょう。

e.g., *Where does she work?*

Warm-Up

1. あなたにとって、怖いものは何ですか？
2. 誰かに何か恩や借りはありますか？

Words and Phrases

CD (Disc 2): Track 30

chap: He's a good chap.

decide: He decided that he will study harder.

owe: I owe you a drink for your help.

decent: get a decent salary

meal: prepare a meal

be mad at: She is mad at me.

beat up: The hero beat up his enemy.

bother: Sorry to bother you.

resources: gather financial resources

turn ... into ...: A magic spell turned a frog into a prince.

nightmare: wake up from a nightmare

end: end a friendship

line of work: In my line of work, I meet many people.

powerful: a powerful company president

dead: a dead animal

return: return home

ruin: a debt that ruined my life

be stuck with: I'm stuck with my horrible boss.

be pleased: I'm really pleased.

be on it: Can somebody finish this project? – Bill's on it.

Script of the Scene

CD (Disc 2): Track 31, 32 / DVD: Chapter 19 (25:52-27:59)

David: I can't believe you still had 20 pounds, and you never said ¹( ) ²( ) about it. Those poor chaps. We left them with stale ³( ).

Olive: The money wasn't ⁴( ). I found it in Marco's pocket. But I decided that after all the things that have happened to you because of me ⁵( ) ⁶( ) I owe you a decent meal.

David: I still need to ask you to give back the ⁷( ) to Murray ..., who is pretty mad at you. You could stop this. He's not like Bill from the pub, ⁸( ) you can beat up when he bothers you. He's got ⁹( ) ¹⁰( ) information about you and the ¹¹( ) to turn your life into a ¹²( ). So please, end this.

Olive: [13](   ) you're in my line of work, [14](   ) always someone powerful who wants you dead. This is what happens [15](   ) you steal from rich people. I can't end this. Not yet. But this could end for [16](   ), Constable Owen. Just go back to [17](   ) [18](   ) and return to your old life.

David: My old life ... you [19](   ) it. There's no returning to anything. I'm stuck with you.

Olive: I'm quite pleased you are.

🕐

David: I [20](   ) [21](   ) to you right now. I'm getting close to her

....

Robert: Gennady? The policeman [22](   ) [23](   ) her. Send your men and kill them both.

Gennady: I'm on it.

Comprehension Check

Exercise 1 Who is David talking to on the phone?

Exercise 2 True (T) or false (F)?

1. (   ) Olive found 20 pounds in Cloutier's pocket.
2. (   ) David thinks that Robert Murray is dangerous.
3. (   ) David will return home.
4. (   ) Robert Murray orders his men to kill both David and Olive.

Exercise 3 Answer the following questions.

1. What did Olive buy for David with 20 pounds?
   (   )
2. What does David ask Olive to return to Robert Murray?
   (   )
3. What does David say Robert Murray can do to Olive?
   (   )
4. Where is David from?
   (   )

Grammar

Relative clauses (*who, whom, which, where, when*)

➔ Used to describe preceding nouns and pronouns	
who	My brother has two classmates. They belong to the baseball club.
	= My brother has two classmates who belong to the baseball club.
	Today's guest is Naomi Osaka. She is a great tennis player.
	= Today's guest is Naomi Osaka, who is a great tennis player.
who(m)	Lincoln was a president. Many people admired him.
	= Lincoln was a president who(m) many people admired.
which	She needs a dress. It is good for today's dance party.
	= She needs a dress which is good for today's dance party.
	They bought the dictionary. Their teacher recommends it.
	= They bought the dictionary which their teacher recommends.
that	My brother has two classmates that belong to the baseball club.
	Lincoln is the President that many people admire.
	She needs a dress that is good for the dance party.
	They bought the dictionary that their teacher recommends.

When + present simple, present simple

➔ Used when you talk about facts and the truth

When you freeze water, it turns into ice.

   (=Water turns into ice when you freeze it.)

When the baby sleeps, the house is quiet.

   (=The house is quiet when the baby sleeps.)

When there is an earthquake, you must not panic.

   (=You must not panic when there is an earthquake.)

Exercise 1 Fill in the blanks with *who, whom,* or *which.*

1. I have many classmates (   ) have traveled abroad.
2. Miki bought a book (   ) is written in Spanish.
3. This is a watch (   ) was given to me by my grandma.
4. Do you know the thief (   ) she mentioned?

Exercise 2 Combine the two sentences with *who, whom,* or *which.*

e.g., *They took a plane. It goes to Paris at noon.*
   → *(They took a plane which goes to Paris at noon.)*

1. Is this the book? You've read it before.
   → (   )
2. I borrowed a book from the library yesterday. It is about planes.
   → (   )
3. I live next to wonderful neighbors. They love having parties.
   → (   )
4. The president hired people. His secretary did not trust them.
   → (   )

Exercise 3 Choose the correct word.

1. When you (boil / heat) water, it (boils / heats).
2. When you (turn / press) this button, the light (turns / presses) on.
3. You (get / mix) water when you (get / mix) hydrogen and oxygen.

Exercise 4 Complete the following sentences.

e.g., *When it's very hot outside, I (**eat ice-cream**).*

1. When there is nothing to eat at home, I (   ).
2. When I am upset, my friend (   ).
3. When I can't sleep at night, I (   ).

TASK: What's the word?

Work in pairs. Person A, look at the four words on page 103. Person B, look at the words on page 105. Take turns describing the words. Continue describing until your partner gets it right.

e.g., *If you have the word "strawberry," you can say:*
　　　It's a fruit that is small.
　　　It's a fruit that is sweet.
　　　It's a fruit which is on short cakes.
　　　It's a fruit which is a type of berry.

Useful Expressions

(a) Describing people
This is a person who ...
These are people who ...
This is a famous person who invented ...

(b) Describing things
It's a thing which ...
It's a thing which you use to ...
It's a fruit that tastes ...
This is a type of machine which ...

Listen and fill in the blanks.

Daiki: You can go first, Jimin.

Jimin: These are people who ₁_____. They are people who

₂_____.

Daiki: I have no idea ...

Jimin: Okay ... let's see. These are people whom you ₃_____ when there is

₄_____.

Daiki: I know! They are ₅_____!

Jimin: Correct! Now it's your turn.

Daiki: This is a type of drink which ₆_____.

Jimin: It's ₇_____!

Daiki: Hahaha. Listen for more clues, Jimin. It's a type of drink which is made from grapes.

Jimin: It's ₈_____!

Daiki: Correct! Wow. You are fast!

[Review 2]

1 Fill in the blanks with the present simple or present continuous form of the verbs in ( ).

e.g., *Don't put the book away, mom. I (**am reading**) it. (read)*

1. She (   ) a word of English. (not understand)

2. I (   ) of buying a house. We are having a baby soon. (think)

3. My son (   ) so loud right now. Usually, he's not like that at all. (be)

4. My friend (   ) singing very much. That's why he often goes to karaoke. (enjoy)

2 Complete the sentences with the nouns in the box. Use *a* or *an* if necessary. You can use each word only once.

bread	chair	~~letter~~	soap	beer	money	music

e.g., *I need to send   **a letter**   to my aunt in Los Angeles.*

1. If you want something in this world, you need to pay (   ).

2. He has been standing there for an hour. Why don't you give him (   ).

3. Many people listen to (   ) when they want to relax.

4. You already had four pints of (   ). Let's go home now.

3 Ask questions with *How many ...?* or *How much ...?* Use the pictures to answer the questions.

e.g., *Question: (How many eggs are there?)*
    Answer: (There are six eggs.)

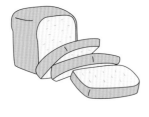

1. Question: ( )
   Answer: ( )

2. Question: ( )
   Answer: ( )

3. Question: ( )
   Answer: ( )

4 **Fill in the blanks with the past simple or past continuous form of the verbs in ( ).**

e.g., We were __washing the dishes__ (wash the dishes) when our mother __came__ (come) home.

1. That night, I _____ (have) dinner when suddenly it _____ (start) snowing.
2. While we _____ (clean), we _____ (hear) a big noise.
3. Mr. Brown _____ (drive) fast when the police officer _____ (stop) him.
4. When the phone _____ (ring), Mary _____ (sleep).

5 **Choose the correct form in ( ).**

e.g., I (bring up / (was brought up)) by Japanese parents in America.

1. This homemade pie (tastes / is tasted) good.
2. The earth (covers / is covered) with land and water.
3. My car (steals / was stolen) from the garage.
4. The city (visits / is visited) by many couples every year.

> **Speaking activity Unit 12**
> Person A's list: Steve Jobs, a police officer, a bicycle, a laptop

103

6 Change the following sentences into the passive voice.

e.g., *My father usually cooks dinner on weekends.*
   → *(Dinner is usually cooked by my father on weekends.)*

1. My grandfather built this house 100 years ago.
   → (   )
2. Somebody has already cleaned this room.
   → (   )
3. They are building a new café near the station.
   → (   )
4. Tom ate the last piece of cake.
   → (   )

7 Choose the correct word.

1. The turtle walked across the bridge very (slow / slowly).
2. I love opera. I think the singers sing so (beautiful / beautifully).
3. He likes saving money. His savings will reach (near / nearly) 1,000,000 dollars.
4. He does not study any subjects very (hard / hardly).

8 Complete the sentences with the comparative or superlative form of the adverbs in ( ).

1. You didn't do very well on the test. You have to study _____ (hard) next time.
2. I have three sisters. The youngest cooks _____ (well).
3. We don't have much time! Please get ready _____ (quickly).
4. Tom won first prize because he ran _____ (fast).

9 Choose the correct form.

1. I (listened / was listening) to music when my brother (came / was coming) to my room.
2. A: What (did you do / were you doing) last night? We were all looking for you!
   B: Sorry, I (played / was playing) video games at a friend's house.

10 Add a question tag to the following sentences.

1. Tom passed his test, (   )?
2. It won't rain today, (   )?
3. Your dog can jump over that fence, (   )?
4. There is no one in the room, (   )?
5. This summer hasn't been humid, (   )?

11 Fill in the blanks with an appropriate *wh*-question word.

1. A: (   ) did you come to Japan?
   B: I came here when I was a child.

2. A: (   ) painted this painting? It's beautiful.
   B: It was painted by Picasso.

3. A: (   ) is Dad? I can't find him anywhere.
   B: He's gone to the supermarket to get dinner.

4. A: (   ) did you have for lunch today?
   B: I had a really delicious plate of spaghetti.

12 Fill in the blanks with *who*, *whom*, or *which*.

1. Is this the girl (   ) you were talking about yesterday?

2. My boyfriend wants a bag (   ) is made in Italy.

3. I have a sister (   ) is going to the U.S. for university next year.

4. Can you translate *Le Petit Prince*, (   ) is written in French?

13 Reorder the words in ( ).

1. A thief is (from / other people / someone / steals / things / who).
   A thief is (   )

2. A museum is (can / a building / art works / you / see / where).
   A museum is (   )

3. A friend is (a person / whom / you / can / trust).
   A friend is (   )

4. The moon is (the earth / moves around / that / an object).
   The moon is (   )

5. A gorilla is (animal / black fur / has / which / a large) and a face.
   A gorilla is (   )

> **Speaking activity Unit 12**
> Person B's list: van Gogh, a hairdresser, a watch, a lemon

オリーブ・グリーン：
ミステリードラマで学ぶ実用英語（CEFR-A2）

検印
省略 　　　©2022年1月31日　第1版発行

編著者　　　　　　　　　　浅利　庸子
　　　　　　　　　　　　　菅野　　悟
　　　　　　　　　　　　　久保　岳夫
　　　　　　　　　　　　　佐藤　亮輔
　　　　　　　　　　　　　SIMPSON William

発行者　　　　　　　　　　原　雅　久
発行所　　　　　　株式会社 朝日出版社
　　　　　　〒101-0065 東京都千代田区西神田 3-3-5
　　　　　　　　電話　東京　(03) 3239-0271
　　　　　　　　FAX　東京　(03) 3239-0479
　　　　　　E-mail　text-e@asahipress.com
　　　　　　　　振替口座　00140-2-46008
　　　　　　　　http://www.asahipress.com/
　　　　　組版／メディアアート　製版／図書印刷